# TAKE YOUR LEADER TO TH_ NEXT LEVEL!

## The 7 Secrets of Thriving Student Leaders

### By Jonathan Sprinkles

*PATRICIA —*
*Your BEST is just*
*around the corner.*
*Eph 3:20*

To _____

From _____

Everyone has an invisible sign hanging from their neck saying,
**"Make me feel important."**
Never forget this message when working with people.
-Mary Kay Ash

For additional information on Jonathan Sprinkles, please visit us on the web at **WWW.JSPRINKLES.COM** or email us at **INFO@JSPRINKLES.COM.**

# I want to hear from you!

Go to **www.JSprinkles.com/testimonials.asp** and leave me a few comments about how this book has helped you and receive a **FREE motivational poster** that will keep you and your group fired up all year long!

# Don't even THINK about having a student success program or leadership retreat without putting "Sprinkles" on it!

❖

Bring Jonathan Sprinkles to your campus to create a customized Success Plan for your group.

To book Jonathan for your next event, go to **WWW.JSPRINKLES.COM** and submit a request. Spaces are limited and usually fill up very quickly, so **ACT NOW!**

# DEDICATION

I dedicate this book to the power of influence and all of the glorious works that we can achieve through it.

This book I also dedicate to my mother, who taught me how to keep my emotional bank accounts in the black by investing in the greatest assets of all—other people.

# CONTENTS

❖

# INTRODUCTION

I'm not big on formalities so, "What's up." Now that we've gotten that out of the way, I'll get straight to it. I can tell you what I'm *not* going to do and what this book *isn't* about. I am not here to talk about how to become a leader. If you're reading this book, you probably already are one. Besides, explaining leadership is like trying to define love; everyone has his own definition based on previous experiences and how much crap they're willing to put up with. As you will see, I don't spend a lot of time discussing boring statistics or philosophically juxtaposing leadership models, either. Yuck and double yuck. This book is a hands-on, action-oriented manual for developing yourself into the best student leader that you can be. After the first few pages, I want you to feel like the information is so relevant that I must have secretly joined your organization when I was doing my research. I believe the French call it déjà vu. In Texas, we just say, "We musta done met somewhere before." So, whether you go cover-to-cover or skip a few chapters, one thing is guaranteed: this Action Guide will make you a much better leader, a more focused student and a purpose-driven person! If you put in the time, you will see some tremendous results. This is my promise to you.

The information in this book will drastically improve your quality of life and the success of your organization. For the sake of your leadership legacy (and your sanity), you need to understand and put into practice the tips that are found in the forthcoming chapters. I promise you, they will make your life a lot easier. That said, now I can tell you what this book is going to do for you.

I created this book to be an accelerated course in student leadership and a solution manual for all of you who are serious about taking your organization's status on campus to the next level. I have only one goal—to help you do it. If you are passionate enough about student leadership to read a book on it, I think you deserve all the time, effort, and heart-felt assistance that you can get. I intend to pour into you all of the tools that will allow you to A) maximize every moment within your organization this school year, B) avoid the all-too-common epidemic of end-of-semester burnout and C) help you get reelected to the same position or even a higher position next year, should you choose to run. I have "been there, done that" and now I want to show you how to "go there and do that," but you will do it much faster and have a lot more fun in the process.

I will be very frank with you, I think I am a great leader and have some phenomenal leadership accolades to my credit. Ironically, I have also exhibited some despicable leadership qualities and have done some things in the name of "leadership" that are embarrassing to me even today. Nobody ever taught me how to handle the pressures of being in the public eye while trying to grow up and find myself as a person at the same time. When I signed up to become a leader, my mentors forgot to mention that everything that I said could and would be used against me in a court of law. They didn't forewarn me about having so many meetings after class that by the time that I got home, studying would be the last thing on my mind, or that I would almost lose my scholarship and fail out of school because of my inability to balance the two worlds. I had to learn all of this the hard way, one teary-eyed lesson at a time. But my pain will be your gain.

Back in the day, I was taught that the best way to make a name for yourself was to "get involved," meaning to become a part of organizations across campus. And involved I became. I joined every club under the sun. As I proved myself through my work ethic, I eventually built up enough credibility to hold positions of authority. My day had finally come. The only catch was that I was there for all the wrong reasons. In no uncertain terms, it was all about me. I had to be seen, be known, be liked, be admired. Because my self-esteem was so low, I perverted the privilege of leadership and used it to show people just how great I was. I treated everything like a zero-sum game: I can only win by making you lose. And I don't like losing! Thus, the motive for my campus involvement was flawed. I used my authority to keep other people down and away from "my" limelight. It was disgusting.
Yes, I am still the same guy that said that he is a great leader.

During my journey, I was broken, humbled, then healed. Being on the border of academic probation was the best and worst thing that ever happened to me. It scared the daylights out of me. It shook out all of the pride that ensnared me for so long. It forced me to become a model student and a servant-leader. I realized that I couldn't do it all myself. I tried and I failed miserably. In the process, I learned some lessons that I still refer to daily. I am so thankful that my turnaround happened before I graduated and I was able to restore most of the relationships that I'd damaged.

So what does this mean for you? No matter where you are or what you've done, there is still a great opportunity for you to be an awesome student leader. Yesterday is now over and today is a new day filled with new chances and new choices. If you have been doing well, you will do even better. If you have been struggling, get ready to turn things around!

I did not invent The *7 Secrets of Thriving Student Leaders,* I discovered them along the way. I do not have a patent on them, but I have simplified them in a manner that you can take and implement immediately. I hope that you take our time together seriously; I certainly do. Be sure to use this book as a reference manual, not a novel. Don't expect to read this once then put it on the shelf. Read it, then read it again. The more you try, the better you'll become.

Before we move on, let me also so say that I am proud of you. I really am. As a student leader, you have volunteered to endure what few could handle. You have been stressed out, over-worked, and struggling to keep your grades up. I bet you're counting the days until the semester is over so that you can ditch this position and flee to safety back at mama's house. I know the feeling. Just know that the things that you are learning now will benefit you for the rest of your life. With every struggle that you endure, you are becoming that much stronger and better equipped to handle anything that life will throw your way. As your adopted big brother, I am looking forward to the many great things that you are going to accomplish, both at school and in life. Go to your destiny!

# SECRET #1: THE 4 DISCIPLINES OF SUCCESSFUL STUDENT LEADERS

❖

I am about to share with you four disciplines that will get your leadership muscles in shape and ready to fight the good fight of faith. I'm going to (in my best Austrian voice) Pump...You Up! Discipline, as it is defined by *Webster's Dictionary*, is *"training expected to produce a specific character or pattern of behavior, especially training that produces moral or mental improvement."* From this definition, you can expect that acquiring these disciplines will make an immediate and significant impact on the output of your leadership. **Student leaders that master the 4 Disciplines ultimately become legends on campus.**

I remember first walking on the yard at the University of Texas, a campus of 53,000 students! I knew that I wanted to show them just how baaaad I was because I had a great run in high school. I thought I was The Bomb.com. Little did I know that I was in for the shock of my lifetime. I heard about what all of the real leaders did on campus and how many faithful supporters they had. I heard stories of sit-ins, petitions and events that drew thousands of people. Though I never met many of the legendary leaders face-to-face, I felt like I knew them through the many stories that were handed down to me. I was instantly humbled. I learned that in order to be great, I had to first do what all the great ones before me did. I had to learn to L.I.V.E. like a real leader.

**L.I.V.E.** Like A Real Leader
**L**eadership = **I**ntegrity + **V**ision + **E**xcellence

## Discipline I — Understanding the Nature of Your Leadership

When I begin a dialogue about leadership, I always start out by stating that I agree wholeheartedly with Dr. John Maxwell's second law in his book *The 21 Irrefutable Laws of Leadership,* which states that "the true measure of leadership is measured by influence–nothing more and nothing less." By definition, influence is *power to sway or affect based on prestige, wealth, ability or position.* Therefore, if you don't play well with others, you can't be a leader no matter how talented you are. Understanding this principle should be the key to unlocking two very important doors for you as a student.

### What's Behind Door #1: The Difference Between Leaders and Individual Contributors

Pick a hero, any hero. Do you think about a fireman rescuing someone from a burning building, your favorite sports star, maybe an armed forces war veteran or even your parents? We often lump all of our most loved people into the "one of the greatest leaders of all time" category, but that's usually only so that we can sell more copies of their life story on DVD (available for free for a limited time with a subscription to *Sports Illustrated*). Now that you know more about what leadership is, let me ask you a quick question; is your hero a leader or an individual contributor? Does she bring out the greatness in others or is she a one-woman-show? Not every high-flying, smooth-talking, death defying son- (or daughter-) of-a-gun is a leader. Some people are great strictly because of their ability to be self-motivated or because their skill level is higher than their peers. But if this level of excellence isn't accompanied by raising the group's overall performance, by getting others to step up their game, these folks are not leaders but individual contributors.

*Here's a great example. Come with me...*
*(Director's note: Begin dream sequence. Queue the harps and the fuzzy screen).* Imagine being in an office about 200 yards long, filled with rows of people occupying hundreds of

cubicles. A computer is on every desk, a person with a head-set on every phone. When you walk in the room during peak hours, the collection of voices resembles a scene from the trading floor on Wall Street. As you walk down each aisle, you can hear glimpses of conversations of all sorts.

"Yes sir, we can do that."

"Ma'am, I think I have exactly what you need."

Or my favorite,

"Let me check with my manager and see if that's okay."

Some people are obviously stressed out. One gentleman's leg is nervously shaking under his desk as he moves through his call. The others look like they are already getting prepared for their vacation as they calmly kick smooth lyrics over the phone like an R&B singer swooning a lady in the front row. They are cooler than a brick of ice. Their feet are up on the desk exposing their Birkenstock sandals, khaki shorts and golf shirt. Everything about them shows relaxation and smooth sailing.

Sometimes you would find these polar opposites sitting across the aisle from each other. From a distance, it looks like some people are on the phone getting news that they just got their ticket into heaven. The others, well...they weren't so fortunate. This was the scene of a typical day at Dell Computer Corporation in the sales call center where I worked. We were a bunch of characters that had the amazing task of having to work together in harmony. The majority of us were young (the average age was well under 35), high-spirited, and we loved recognition, especially in front of a large group. I was quick-ly promoted to one of the "elite" sales groups tasked with closing the big deals. If you wanted to see what ego, steroids and caffeine would do when mixed together, my group would have made a great case study. We were B-A-D and we knew it—and wanted everyone to know it, too. If you sent us over to the Middle East, we may not have won any wars, but we darn sure would have made sure that our names were spelled correctly in *USA Today*. You get the picture.

The irony of the situation is that my group of Senior Sales Reps was (theoretically) looked at first when management positions opened up. The challenge was to find someone who could stop beating their chest saying, "Me, me, me" and learn how to say, "We, we, we." In short, the hiring staff had to sift through all of the individual contributors and try to pick those with leadership potential. In the interviews, they would first ask to see our sales numbers, then make sure that we understood the business inside and out. Finally, they gave us the kicker. They would inquire about specific instances in which we contributed to someone else's success besides our own. Had we coached or mentored anyone? Had we created any new processes to simplify or enhance the way that we did business? The underlying message was, "We know you've got game, but who else's game is better because you're here? What else can you show us besides your individual accolades?" The "what else" is the key differentiator between a leader and an individual contributor. The individual contributors like the spotlight. Leaders take the light and turn it into a lighthouse, using it to guide others.

The "what else" is servant-leadership, a concept coined by Robert Greenleaf, the founder of The Center for Servant-Leadership. Here is an excerpt taken from the *Servant As Leader* published by Robert Greenleaf in 1970:

> Servant-leadership is a practical philosophy which supports people who choose to serve first, and then lead as a way of expanding service to individuals and institutions. Servant-leaders may or may not hold formal leadership positions. Servant-leadership encourages collaboration, trust, foresight, listening, and the ethical use of power and empowerment.

Greenleaf also adds, "The servant-leader is servant first...It begins with the natural feeling that one wants to serve, to serve first. Then conscious choice brings one to aspire to lead."

**The door to your next level of leadership is going to be opened by helping other people walk through theirs.**

## What's Behind Door #2: Leadership is an equal-opportunity employer

This should be a very exciting thought for young leaders. What this should tell you is that your career as a great leader starts RIGHT NOW! I don't care if you don't currently hold a position in your organization. If Sue Ellen is the president but everyone looks at you (and not Sue Ellen's big-headed self) before they vote yes or no, guess what—YOU are the leader! Have you ever been in a class where the teacher (the formal leader) had less control over the students than the class clown (the influential leader)? Exactly. When influence is the measuring stick, the playing field levels and everyone has the same shot at obtaining the group's favor. Who cares if they said you're too young? It's about influence. Who cares if you didn't get voted in? It's about influence. So, if the name of the game of influence, how do you get more of it? I'm glad you asked. **Leadership is measured by influence. Influence is gained by earning trust.**

## LEADERSHIP ⟫➡ INFLUENCE ⟫➡ TRUST

This sounds like a perfect place for a quote by a smart, dead person, but I will resist the temptation. Without trust, it is nearly impossible for your members to freely allow you to take them through uncharted territory. Stop and think for a moment, don't the people that you trust the most (I mean the ones you would trust with your internet passwords) have the greatest amount of influence in your life? You could have your mind made up about going in one direction, but if they say, "I wouldn't do that if I were you," you'd stop in your tracks. They have your best interest at heart, they know what they're talking about and they seem to be right far more than they are wrong. Keeping this as simple as possible, if you seek to grow your leadership, work on getting people to trust you. Here's how, L.I.V.E. like a real leader.

## Discipline II — Living With High Integrity

My definition of integrity is *consistency through and through.* It is a strict adherence to a moral and ethical code, no matter the circumstances. Why are morals, ethics and consistency so important? Keep reminding yourself what this is all about— trust; and **when it comes to trust, more is *caught* than is *taught.*** People will learn much more about you by what they *catch* you doing when you think that nobody is looking than they will from the words that you speak from the front of the room. Your group has to know beyond a shadow of a doubt that they can believe in you to represent yourself and your members with the same standard at all times. If they trust you, they are placing their faith in you, they believe in you. Your cynical side may say, "Come on, is integrity *really* this deep? Does anyone really care?"

Let me answer that question with a question, would you like to have a spouse that is faithful to you *most* of the time? Why then should someone believe in you if you are only *partially* honest with them? Earning and keeping trust means that people have to believe in who you are, which will speak more loudly than what you've done.

I will never forget one of the greatest character-building challenges that I have faced in my life was when I was emceeing a seminar long ago. All of the platform speakers were friends of mine and they were there strictly because of our relationship. By nature, I am a very playful person, especially when I am on stage. This time though, I clearly went too far. As I was introducing one of my friends, I made a joke about her that was funny, but inappropriate. Had I made a similar jest after the talk, it would have been seen as good fun. What I did though was dig a hole for her that she had to climb out of during her talk. Gosh, even thinking about it now makes me cringe because I feel so bad. She was doing me a favor, and I did her wrong.

To make a long story short, I called her the next day and said, "I really messed up. That intro was wack and someone brought it to my attention that it wasn't received in the spirit that it was intended. It in absolutely no way represented the level of admiration and respect that I have for you. Even though I did say publicly that I was just joking, I still want to personally apologize for my bad judgment. I'm sorry."

She both acknowledged my sincerity and was appreciative of my willingness to be a man about my mistakes. She accepted my apology, we smoothed things out and went on to become even better friends. Actually, we'll be working together again soon. I will be making a guest appearance next year in a movie that she's shooting with Tom Cruise. Nah, not really, but it would make a real nice ending, wouldn't it?

To further illustrate the importance of integrity, let's look at what happens on a larger scale. When Enron, a large energy company, fell due to an internal accounting scandal, both the company and its accounting firm were blamed for one of the greatest stock market drops of our era. Why? Enron wasn't the largest company on the market. They were only one of many. How could one company's downfall create such a domino effect in the market? One word, my friend: trust. The world lost faith in America's Big Business policies. Stockholders' attitudes were, "If they got caught, *who else* has been stealing money?" The witch-hunt was on. Everybody was instantly under the microscope. Large companies spent millions of public relations dollars saying, "That was them, not us!" They had to work hard to regain the trust of a betrayed public.

If you have ever caught someone cheating or stealing, your first thought is being glad that you caught them and then, like clockwork, the second thought drifts to, "Hmm...I wonder how many other times this has happened in the past." Is integrity and consistency really this deep? Absolutely, yes!

If you are a high-profile student leader, you have to accept that your life will change in many ways. You are in a fishbowl where everyone watches you at all times; from the cafeteria, to the classroom, to the parking lot. Just as celebrities lose their privacy, you too will be the subject of wanted and unwanted attention. You are on a pedestal, seen as being higher than most. Rational people know that this is unfair, but it's something that you just have to deal with. Even more so, some people will make it their business to knock you down off your pedestal and show others that you aren't all that people make you out to be. I believe that the proper terminology for them in the urban lexicon is (let the congregation say it together) *haters*! **Haters will come after your character in an attempt to crush people's ability to trust in you. When you are a first-class student leader, you can't afford to give them any ammunition.** I am in no way asserting that you should live to appease your critics. I am saying, however, that you can not ignore the double standards and risk all that is at stake simply because you stubbornly refuse to be mindful of your surroundings.

Student leaders have to be the same person day in and day out. We have to be the same on stage as we are behind closed doors. Being "sometimey" won't get it. Your members have to be able to know that if you say you'll be there at 6:00 pm, when 6:00 pm comes rolling around, you are ready to get started. If and when your integrity comes into question, people need to be able to say, "She has been an honest person as long as I have known her, so I don't have any reason to question her character." Now *that's* a reputation.

Let's just keep it real for a second. Nobody here has gone a day without making a mistake. We all mess up sometimes. So, how should we rebound from our falls? It's easier than we think. We apologize. We apologize frequently. We apologize sincerely. If we don't freak out about our mistakes, other people will. **We have to learn how to mess up, fess up, then get up.** Acknowledge the shortfall, pledge not repeat it, then don't do it again. Just be real with your people and admit your mistakes. They will see your sincerity and forgive you as an imperfect person trying to do the best that you can. The only times that we don't deserve forgiveness are when we aren't truly sorry or still strive to maintain an image of being perfect, even after our indiscretions. There are too many other people who are hungry for the opportunity to lead for folks to sit around and listen to another round of your, "Please give me another chance. I'm gonna get my act together" speech. Sometimes you just can't put enough perfume on a pig to make it smell sweet. Just be humble, get through it and *move on*!

Final note on integrity: **as a leader, your reputation is your most valuable asset**. There is a proverb that says, "A good name is to be chosen over silver and gold." There will be a time where you will need someone's good words about you to get into or out of something. There are some things that money just can't buy. Your respect is definitely one of them. It is, as MasterCard would say, "Priceless."

## Discipline III — Walking With a Vision

The famous author and philosopher William Arthur Ward once declared, "Without having a dream, you will never have a dream come true." Your dream come true is your personal vision for your group coming to pass.

Vision, as I define it in my book *Why Settle?*, is "disclosure of an unseen reality." The person with the most compelling plan to take the group to the Promised Land is the one that people will gravitate toward. It is the person who shows the most confidence, as though they have already walked the path before. If you and I went on a trip to your hometown, I would happily hand over the keys and allow you to get us to our destination because you are familiar with the territory. I could trust you to get us around without needing map or getting us lost in some rough neighborhood where thugs with baseball bats will treat the car like it was a piñata.

During the last days of Walt Disney's life, a man came to see him. The guy sat by his bed and said, "Oh Walt, it's so terrible that you're not going to see Epcot Center when it's finished being built at Disney World." Walt's face got serious. He stared back at the man and said, "Are you kidding me? If I hadn't first seen it in my mind, you never would have seen it with your eyes."

We talk highly about the term vision, but how does one acquire and hone his vision? It's much easier than you may think. Simply engage your creative mind, propel your thinking and reverse engineer the desired outcome. In plain English, mentally beam yourself into the future, placing yourself in the circumstances that you want to be and ask yourself, "What did I have to do to get here?" For example, if your vision is to double the meeting attendance from 20 people to 40 people, imagine the room jam-packed with 40 people. See as much detail as possible. See the smiles, the side-chatter, the people eagerly taking notes from the guest speaker Jonathan Sprinkles' awesome lecture. Make your vision as vivid as possible. Now ask, "How did I make this reality?" You implemented one of the promotional campaigns that you read in this book, you called on five professors who had their classes attend for extra credit, you submitted a press release to the school newspaper to drum up excitement, you asked the local pizza shop to donate food and you made one of the best choices of you college career— bringing in Jonathan Sprinkles to speak.

When you create a vision then think backwards, you gain confidence and momentum, feeling like it has already happened. You just have to figure out how to make it so that others can see it, too. I am sure that Epcot started out as something that people at first told Walt Disney, "No way. Too much. Too big. Too expensive." But Walt had already been there. He had already walked inside of its silver dome. He had tasted the food from the many countries. Walt had already spent too much time in the park to believe other people's doubts about whether it could exist.

In the same way that Walt Disney went there, you can go there for your group. **Write down the vision so that your people see it, know it and most importantly, live it!**

## Discipline IV — Possessing A Standard of Excellence

Excellence is being the best YOU that YOU can be. It's a personal thing. Excellence doesn't always mean being the best in the group. It means being better than yesterday's personal best. **Excellence is when you challenge your limitations or beliefs about how well you can do.** It is that burning desire to be just a little wiser, more patient, more innovative, better prepared, more articulate, healthier, happier and more focused than you were yesterday. Please don't confuse what I am saying about excellence as a plea for you to be perfect. Only the Creator is perfect, but we can all be excellent.

I can't trust someone to lead me if she doesn't operate with a spirit of excellence. If she tolerates starting late, shabby publicity, last-minute preparation and excuse-ridden performances, that is a big red flag for me. Maybe it sounds shallow or judgmental, but I even pay attention to my leader's style of dress and how she treats her car and her home. These are often tell-tale signs about one's standard of excellence. If she will put up with walking around in wrinkled clothes or driving around with old hot sauce packets from Taco Bell under the floor mats, I have a hard time believing that she lives with excellence elsewhere in her life. Do you remember what we just discussed about integrity, consistency, and more being caught than taught? This is where it comes to play.

Before we move on, I want to draw a line in the sand right here and make sure that you understand what I am saying. I am not concerned about what kind of clothes, car or house people have. I do, however, pay close attention to how well they treat their stuff. Trust me, pressed Levis look better than wrinkled Gucci any day.

Think of excellence as constant personal development. We all love to be around people that are highly motivated, enthusiastic and have a passion for seeing progress. Don't the people who influence you the most always challenge you to get better at doing what you do? Don't they light your fire when they say inspirational statements like," I believe in you" and "You can do this?" With that in mind, let's shift our focus toward how your spirit of excellence will enhance those that you influence.

Tiger has one. Madonna has had a few. Ozzy has several even today. What am I referring to? A coach. Those that have achieved success have utilized the services of someone who could inspire them to dig deeper and find their greatness within. Regardless of how many accolades they have already achieved and how much money they make, they are still in pursuit of the next great achievement in their life. They know that their talent is only potential until their coach helps them make it reality.

And of course, you dynamic leader you, your job is to be the miner of your members' hidden talents. Not in a "you need to step up if you're going to hang around me" kind of way, but in the supportive, "believing in the beauty within every person" kind of way. **If you obsess over helping the people around you achieve their dreams and discovering their most excellent selves, you will not only be liked and trusted, you will be forever remembered as the person that future leaders seek to emulate.** Stop right here and ask yourself who in your organization could benefit from learning just one thing that you do well. Make a short list below.

| Member | What can I help them with? |
|--------|---------------------------|
|        |                           |
|        |                           |
|        |                           |
|        |                           |
|        |                           |

As you humble yourself and serve others, you will move from success to significance. As my best friend taught me, "The greatest among us must be the servants of all."

## How to Elevate Your Level of Excellence

Read-Read books on leadership, customer service, fundraising, philosophy, management or anything that will teach you how to be a more dynamic leader. Leaders are readers!

Keep a journal-Record your thoughts about victories and challenges. Be sure to write down the biggest obstacles each week and what you are doing to overcome them. This will keep you focused and will provide a great reference for future leadership. Keep this in mind at all times—**the greatest indicator of your leadership is not what happens while you're there, but what happens once you're gone.** Your journal will be a key building block in creating a lasting legacy.

Connect with a mentor-Get a hardcore mentor. If you just want someone to stroke your ego and tell you that everything is going to be okay, go see one of the counselors at the student health center. What you need is someone who will congratulate you when it's due and also put your butt in check when it's necessary. There is wisdom in experience. Gain insights from other people's mistakes rather than waiting to make your own.

Start a friendly competition-Find another leader on campus with a lot of ambition, even if he or she is older or more experienced than you are. Tell him or her that you want to start a friendly wager (the prize doesn't have to be money) to see whose group can achieve more of its goals. The synergy that you two will create will have you running circles around other leaders on campus.

My buddy Austin and I had such a competition that we both ended up being selected for the highest leadership award that they give at the University of Texas. We admired, supported and challenged each other every step of the way. To this day, his hustle has continued. I am very proud of him. He is currently the highest-ranking African American official in his company. But being that I own my own business, I guess I am the highest-ranking African American official in my company, too. So *there* Austin! Just kidding, bro.

Make time to be great–Most of us are so busy we don't know what to do. All of the Palm Pilots and cell phones in the world don't seem to be enough to keep us from feeling overwhelmed, over-worked and under-appreciated. But you've got to carve a little time out each day to sit, observe and strategize. If you are always doing and never planning, your leadership will diminish from being pro-active to reactive. Even with the best intentions, if you are not assessing your growth, you are bound to go down like countless leaders before you. Unplug the phone, push back from your desk and just "be." Relax a little. Focus on the possibilities, not the harsh realities. Give your mind and body a chance to recharge so that when you step back in the game, you'll be ready to go full steam ahead for another four quarters.

Osmosis–Hang around people who have what you want. If you need to learn how to dress, find the most "jiggy" people that you can. If you need to improve your public speaking skills, put yourself around the articulate people. Whatever you need, get it through your network. **Association creates assimilation.**

Set greatness goals–Pin up on your wall the top five competencies that you want to develop by the end of the semester and what these skills are going to do for your life. Make them the first thing that you see in the morning and the last thing that you see at night. The more that you focus on them, the greater your chances of achieving them.

For bonus points, here's a short list of additional characteristics that is specifically geared toward student leadership. Study this list and see which skills you possess and which skills you still need to develop within yourself.

**7 More Very Important Student Leadership Qualities That You Probably Didn't Think Of...But Still Need to Know**

## 1. Supportive

Prejudge no one. Encourage everyone. When it's time to reprimand, do it in private. When it's time to praise, do it in public. When your people aren't being paid, they are working for recognition, pride and appreciation for what they do. *Show them some love!*

## 2. Respectful

It takes maturity to respect everyone's point of view. If you want to develop a culture that recognizes everyone as a valued source of input, the leader must begin by holding everyone in the highest regard. In student-run organizations, you are going to find people of all types, sizes and temperaments. Not everyone will take well to jokes or playful comments. It is a must that you carry the torch of respect for the whole group. If you're wondering how much disrespect you should tolerate within the group, as James Brown said, "Don't start none, won't be none." That's right, zero-tolerance. Always take the high road and demand that others do the same. You'll never regret that decision.

## 3. Focused

Keep your eyes on the prize. When the going gets tough, tough leaders get going. They keep everyone looking at the big picture, not the distractions that slow us down along the way. Don't get caught up in the limelight. Always stay humble. When you are truly focused, you don't mind sharing the glory as long as it can inspire others to buy into the goal. Your greatest happiness should come from seeing those that you have developed shine just as brightly as you do. It's not about you anyhow. It's about the mission, not the missionary. Focus on getting to the finish line, not who gets the most applause during the race.

## 4. Charismatic

Great leaders have a personality that is magnetic. Their personality exudes energy. They make other people feel better about themselves when they are around them. They bring the best out of others and seek to highlight people's best qualities.

## 5. Resourceful

As a student leader, you know what it's like to have champagne wishes and a Ramen Noodle budget. Your resourcefulness and creativity are your two greatest assets in overcoming your cash-flow-challenged bank account and still pull off great programs. There are always untapped resources on campus and in the community. Most schools actually have people and programs that are designed to help students. Oftentimes, these people *never get used*. They are literally waiting to have someone ask them for assistance because they have to prove that they are helping a certain number of students in order to keep their jobs. Find these people! The legendary leaders learn to use what they have in order to get everything they want.

## 6. Hard-headed

I mean this in a good way. You must develop a thick skin when it comes to taking criticism. If you are going to whimper and cry when people and problems come your way, you need to sit down and let someone with some you-know-what take your place.

## 7. Self-Starter

Immortal student leaders don't wait for things to happen, they make things happen. They don't wait for things to fall in their laps. Nobody has to tell them to get up and do something. Leaders see a void and they seek to fill it and will stay until the job is done.

As a final note, I feel the need to stand up for you like a big brother before a big fight at the bike racks. I know that as tough as it is to stand up and be a leader, there are people out there who make our jobs ten times harder because they have problems seeing you make it while they fake it. I have written this last piece just for you.

### *Dealing with the Haters*

As a leader, you have to accept that people will be gunning for you, looking to poke holes in your abilities, intelligence and even your character. No, it's not right. No, it shouldn't be that way. Nevertheless, it's a fact of life. People will watch your success, congratulate you to your face, and hate on you behind your back, dripping with jealousy. You will hear a lot of "She thinks she's all that" or "He's so conceited." For some, you are a constant reminder of what they could have had if they had not given up along the way. Although they appear to be upset with you, they are really upset with the fact that you have everything they want: success, admiration, influence, confidence, discipline, and a great reputation...*and you have the nerve to look good in the process!* You just continue to stand firm, knowing that you're doing the right thing by walking in Truth. Don't let anyone's small-minded insults get you off your game. On campus and in life, someone will always be upset with your success. **You *must* be bigger than your critics!**

Don't feel the need to change so that people who don't like you will stop talking about you. Pay attention, *they don't like you!* If your success ticks them off, they'll really have a field day if you fail. Be who you are, not who they want you to be. **Don't settle for someone else's opinion of what you can and can't do.** They don't know you like that! They have seen what you *have done*, but they don't know what you *can do*. One of the saddest things that occurred in my life and that I see in the lives of many other high-performance leaders is that we choose to conform to a lower standard just so that other people won't talk about us. What a tragedy! All of that potential is locked up and stored away on the shelf, never to be brought to the world. Marvin Winans said it best, "As long as you don't think you're anything, you'll be just that. As long as you think you're going to fail, you'll accomplish it every time." Who cares about what they say about you? What do YOU say about you?

My friend, the only way to conquer this fear is to develop an unshakable understanding of who YOU are. You couldn't convince Picasso that he was born to be a pastry chef. You couldn't convince Shaquille O'Neal that he was meant to be a jockey. You couldn't convince Britney Spears that she was supposed to be a preacher's wife. So, why do we allow others to influence our thinking about our importance to the group? My colleague came up with a powerful saying that I often repeat to myself in tough times. He said, "I use lies and criticism as a sign that I'm getting closer to the goal. I believe in the principle that algebra taught us: a negative times a negative equals a positive. So, if a negative person says negative things about me that must mean that I'm on the right track!" **If someone tries to rain on your parade, just grab and umbrella and keep marching, baby!**

## How to be a REAL Leader

Losers see obstacles; leaders see opportunities.

Losers make mistakes; leaders make discoveries.

Losers get jealous; leaders get inspired.

Losers player hate; leaders congratulate then emulate.

Losers say, "maybe," leaders say, "must."

Losers retreat; leaders regroup.

Losers complain; leaders confront.

Losers pout; leaders pray.

Losers react; leaders respond.

Losers focus on what has been; leaders dream about what can be.

Losers talk about the good ol' days; leaders believe that the best is yet to come!

*© Jonathan Sprinkles, 2004*

# SECRET #2: HOW TO SPOT POTENTIAL LEADERS...AND PUT THEM TO WORK!

❖

If not knowing a good thing when it comes our way was a crime, we'd all be locked up and doing hard time. It is sad to see how many bright, enthusiastic, talented and eager students end up leaving our organizations. Some leave by force, some by choice. How do we let these people slip through our fingers and lose them to other organizations? How do we allow those with great leadership potential go from highly- involved to totally uninvolved? At orientation, we do our best to get them to join our organizations, but somewhere between the first day of school and mid-semester, we stop feeding their interests and they choose to go elsewhere. This makes less sense than a bird flying backwards. What's the deal? I'll tell you what's happening. We as leaders get on the Complain Train and gripe about the type of people that we don't want, but we don't have a clue about how to recognize the ones that we do want.

I learned this lesson the hard way not too long ago during a trip to Wally World (most people know this place as Wal-Mart). Is it me, or is Wal-Mart just the coolest place to be between the hours of 2:00-4:00 am? And don't let it be a Wally World Supercenter! I may be there all night! I'll throw on my Wally World uniform (sweats, a t-shirt, old tennis shoes and a cap...pulled down low) and wander around for hours on end. I have been known to cruise each and every aisle, just because it's Wally World and that's what you do at Wally World. That's right, I'm not scared to admit that I'll put on those big headphones and listen to every CD in the music section, even the ones in Spanish. On a good trip, I've been known to go down the dog food aisle...and I don't even have a dog! I just love putting things in my cart. I'll even buy panty hose if I can find them on a good sale. Okay, maybe that's TMI (too much information). Who needs amusement parks or movies when you have Wally World? Heck, who needs *school* when you have Wally World!

Anyhow, I was on what was supposed to be a routine trip for just one item, but because I was on my cell phone the entire time, I made the error of not writing down the item that I was going to get. Big mistake! My conversation was really good, so it took up the majority of my focus. Totally losing time as I became more deeply engaged in the conversation, I walked around the store like it was a cross-country marathon. I went from corner to corner, from the meat section to the fertilizer. Though I was very impressed with the recently rolled back prices, I still didn't have what I came for. Then it hit me...I DIDN'T EVEN *KNOW* WHAT I CAME FOR! I screamed like Macaulay Culkin in *Home Alone*. I had no clue what I was doing or why I was standing in that section. I felt like I had just looked in *Men In Black's* little red light. I said, "Hold on, I know that came here to get something, but I have no clue what I was supposed to get." I could have been staring at it face-to-face and wouldn't have known it.

I was so embarrassed that I put down the stuffed giraffe, the porcelain rooster and the neon license plate holder, got in my car and went home. Of course, as soon as I sat on my couch, I remembered what I needed, batteries for my TV remote. But it was too late. I was doomed, forced to spend the rest of my shameful evening watching reruns of *Reading Rainbow* because I was too miserable to get up and change the channel.

Have you ever felt like this before (well, minus the rooster and *Reading Rainbow*)? You know what I mean. Have you ever felt like you could have been staring at exactly what you needed and didn't know it? Well, chances are, there are probably several cash cows that you've been overlooking within your group that you have yet to milk...uh, motivate into becoming one of your star members. Before I knew how to spot potential leaders, I was always losing good people to other leaders that could. New members would join my group, hang around for a little while, get bored and eventually join another organization that took a special interest in them and got them involved quickly in his group. They would go elsewhere and flourish, leaving me to wonder, "What about me?" It was like sitting in the dark, watching the captain of the football team dance with your prom date all night long. Not that that happened to me or anything. Let's face it, while everyone has the potential to become a leader on some level, most people are fully content with not living up to their potential, especially not their leadership potential. It is such a huge responsibility, many students would much rather sit back and let other people do the work.

In your organization, there will be two very important groups of people that you need to spot as quickly as possible: Spark Plugs and Gas Guzzlers. While Spark plugs get things started, gas guzzlers drain the life out of you. Spark plugs are full of positive energy and potential. Guzzlers are full of...uh, not positive energy. They are quick to point out what's wrong, but they never do anything to help the situation. While the rest of the group is working, they spend their time talking, filling others with doubt and negativity. Instead of pitching in to help, they are the type that will say, "See, I told you that we never should have done this in the first place." When you have guzzlers in your group, you feel like you're raising a child. A problem child!

So, how can you tell the difference between someone who could become a leader if he had enough mentoring and someone who is ready to lead right now? Along with the leadership qualities that we have discussed in the previous chapters (I didn't include those for nothing, you know), through my research, I have discovered five traits of a member that is ready to step up to be a leader.

---

### A Spark Plug:
**Shows the desire to be a leader.**
You have to want to be a good leader in order to be a good leader. It sure doesn't happen by accident. **Don't ever appoint people to leadership unless they want to be a leader.** If you do, you will find that they will be more trouble than they're worth. For example, some campuses have a shortage of men who want to get involved, so the women will find anyone with "outdoor plumbing" and try to rope him into group membership. This never works because his motivation is not for the club; it's for the relationship with the woman that

brought him into the group. When things aren't fun anymore, those that are forced into leadership are the first ones to go AWOL. Unless they say, "I want to be a leader," don't bother them about it until it's their time.

During your orientation process, ask how many in the group actually want to become leaders. Then ask them why and make them tell you what they can bring to the table. Write it down! This will give you a great inventory of who is serious and who isn't. Don't go on a Blair Witch hunt when you have willing and able people right in your face. These, my friend, are your Spark Plugs.

### Steps up when others sit down.

This is a HUGE sign! Certain people have a knack for doing whatever has to be done, no matter the task. If you have someone in your group that is doing things *without being told* or going the extra mile to make sure that things turn out right, you've got a leader on your hands. These folks will be very easy to find even in a large group because most of your members will be socializing and playing around, but your Spark Plugs are focused, looking for something to do. The next time that your group gets together, sit back and observe who does what. These, my friend, are your Spark Plugs.

### Stays consistent under pressure

Sometimes the term "student leader" doesn't accurately describe the way that things really go down. Because we are pulled in so many directions, we end up being more like leader, employee, referee, boyfriend, counselor, and oh yeah, student. We have to hold many hats and wear them all successfully. The strain has brought even the toughest men and women to their knees. I was one of them. However, there are those rare birds that can handle the pressure of multitasking and still remain as cool as a cucumber. These are special people. I have friends who have gone to school full-time, worked full-time and still managed to be some of the most dedicated club members that we have ever seen. I don't know how they do it, but they sure do it with grace. They make great role models and earn the respect and admiration of their peers very quickly. If they can display time management well enough to handle such responsibility, they obviously have the type of work ethic that you want around you. These, my friend, are your Spark Plugs.

## Solves problems
Before you get to know potential leaders, you may consider them cocky or brash because of the confidence that they possess in their ability to solve problems. I remember one year in particular when a freshman attended one of our organization's meetings and wrote a two-page paper with detailed suggestions on how we could run our meetings better! Though it seems funny at first, when you put your ego aside, this is a person who is obviously very analytical by nature and has an eye for improvement. By the way, typing a two-page paper takes more than a couple of minutes, so he wasn't afraid to put in some action behind his thoughts. When we put our egos aside, we realized that this person had some potential!

Spark Plugs take on meeting the need as a personal challenge. If necessary, they will get very creative in order to accomplish the task. They don't have big egos, and wouldn't consider themselves too good to do something as small as putting the chairs back in order when the meeting is over when others have carelessly filed filed out without thinking about the room's condition. The Spark Plugs in the group see what needs to be done and they hop to it. The next time there is a piece of paper on the floor or a volunteer opportunity, pay attention to who takes on the chore. That, my friend, is your Spark Plug.

## Sees the job through to its completion
If you have heard the expression, "Winners don't quit and quitters don't win," the same is true for leaders. How cool is it to know that you can put something in someone's hand and it's actually going to...get done! I am convinced that some people are just lazy. About half-way through anything they start, they begin to look for excuses why they can't finish it. They habitually put themselves in this position, either due to a

lack of desire or a lack of discipline. They refuse to follow through and they are fine with it. Spark Plugs are much different. They assume a sense of ownership about their project and will stay up for two days straight if that's what it takes to get it done. I can't explain it, that's just how they are! Their word is their bond, so if they say that they'll get it done, you can rest assured that it's money in the bank. If you have people in your organization that are unfailingly true to their word, these, my friend, are your Spark Plugs.

### You down with OPP? You should be!

Spark Plugs are rare gems and should be treated with high regard. Pareto's Principle is also known as The 80/20 Rule. It states that 80 percent of the work will be done by 20 percent of the people. The Spark Plugs are that 20 percent. It makes a lot of sense to devote as much time to developing them as you can. Any investment in a Spark Plug is an investment in your group's future. The Gas Guzzlers won't produce much for you, so investing all of your time in getting them to act right doesn't make much sense. The more you invest in your Spark Plugs, the more secure your club's future will be. **Invest your dollar time in Spark Plugs and your penny time in Gas Guzzlers.**

---

### What exactly do you need to do?

When you find Spark Plugs, you need to give them some **O.P.P.:**

Give them as many **OPPORTUNITIES** to get involved as they can handle.

> Pull them into their stretch zone. Share your duties with them so they will already have experience serving in your position when they take it over. This will also lighten your load a bunch...whew!

**POUR** into them all of your knowledge, resources and contacts. Invest your best in them. Make sure that by the time you leave your position, you have introduced them to every worthwhile leader, faculty member, and business owner that you know. Teach them all of your tricks. Spill the beans. Let the cat out of the bag. For a Spark Plug, it's worth it!

**PRAISE** them often.

Affirm them through their odd and complex times. There is no such thing as growth without growing pains. You have to be their #1 fan through this process, assuring them that as soon as they catch on, they will be on top of the world. It's up to you to make sure that they don't slack off or even worse, quit.

So, now you know how to find and how to treat Spark Plugs. That's it, right? Almost. If you have one in your care, you need to know specifically which traits to develop within them and how to put them to work in a manner that will produce the greatest results. Let's continue with our study.

## The 4 Sources of a Student Leader's Power

### 1. Wealth

I learned in finance class that the #1 rule of finance is that Cash is King. This rule is valid in organizations as well. It's valid on planet Earth. If you have money, you will be able to buy yourself a little notoriety. Be it a nice car, stylish clothes or laid out apartment, having money is always a plus when it comes to getting people's attention. However, wealth can be deceiving. If you have money and other people don't, you're only of value to them if you are willing to share your wealth with them. Thus, if you cut off their supply of money, they will cut you out of the loop. In a student leader's world, your power must be more far-reaching than your Visa's credit limit if you want lasting results. **Money will get you noticed, but it won't get you respect.**

### 2. Opinion

On every campus, there is a class clown. There is always that guy or girl who talks loud and has a group of people around, almost like a group of followers who enjoy being entertained by his or her antics. Because of their charisma, they often possess the ability to sway the public opinion in their favor by being louder, funnier or more boisterous than the rest. The down side of this personality type is that these people are rarely taken seriously and are usually presumed to be unintelligent or disinterested in important issues. They are often watched, but rarely respected. They are seen as a source of entertainment, not enlightenment.

## 3. Relationships

This is the strongest form of power that a student leader can have. What have we been talking about for this entire book, *relationships*! Relationships are what make the difference between ordinary and extraordinary. **Having a strong character and a winning reputation cannot be purchased nor persuaded, it must be earned.** Once a strong relationship is established, it is a tie that no outside force can sever. Relational power is the greatest power of all.

## 4. Knowledge

What you know is a power that comes second only to who you know. If you are the only person in your group that knows how to maintain the web page or who has access to the group's bank account, you have positioned yourself through your knowledge as a resource. It is nearly impossible to do without a resource because you need it for your existence. Air and water are resources. How long could we go without them? The more you educate yourself about the tasks that are critical to the functionality of your organization, your power will increase proportionately. They won't just want you, they'll need you.

Now that we know what W.O.R.K.s, its finally time to insert the Spark Plugs into the system. What normally happens is we love on them at first, but because of our bureaucracy, we end up losing them. They never get to have any hands-on experience because they're not ranked high enough to qualify for "meaningful" work. This is the limitation of the Traditional Organizational Structure. It is designed to keep the Executive Board on top, even if their work ethic is the pits. Members that are not on the Executive Board but are very dedicated are not rewarded for their commitment because they lack the power to make decisions where it counts. What this model says to the members is that position is more important than participation. Thus, no matter how hard members try, their only solution to creating change is "wait until next year." How many 'next years' do you think someone will take before they find another group that will appreciate them immediately?

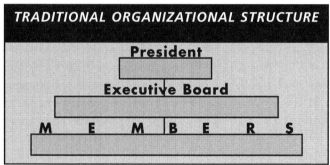

TRADITIONAL ORGANIZATIONAL STRUCTURE

President

Executive Board

M  E  M  B  E  R  S

A solution to this problem is to reorganize your group into what is called a Meritocracy, where you are judged by your merit, or your works. This way, there is a heightened emphasis on contributing to the group, not just holding an office. In a Meritocracy, in order to get things done, you are forced to utilize other people, so you have to be kind to them and appreciate their input. In a Traditional Organization, the most important person is the President. In a Meritocracy, who is the most important person? The one who *contributes* the most! This model is more fair to everyone across the board and is a symbol of the club's belief in valuing every member's input. For the sake of order, in a Meritocracy, you will still have an Executive Board. But in this case, members will be rewarded for their labor, not for their status alone. Everything is earned, not granted. **If nothing is granted, nothing can be taken for granted.**

I have borrowed the titles that Rick Warren uses in his book

*The Purpose-Driven Church* to explain how churches and other volunteer organizations operate. I will explain:

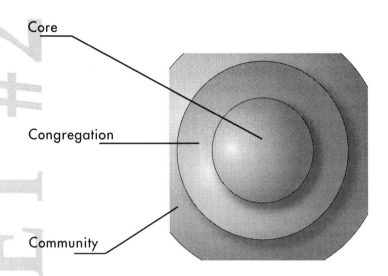

Core

Congregation

Community

**Core**- Your most committed group. They refer to the group as "my organization" because of their sense of ownership and love for it. They log the most hours in meetings, planning events and working at events. The core members are the ones that you know are going to not only show up, but also be there early to set up and stay late to clean up. The core is the smallest but most obvious group because they are always around. They take a personal interest accompanied by an active role in the success of the organization and seek to develop better skills so that they can make the entire group better. Their primary concern is taking the club to the next level.

**Congregation**- A slightly larger and still very useful group. Without the manpower (and yes, womanpower) of the congregation, most of the group's programs wouldn't happen. Those in the congregation are committed to being a member of the group, but occasionally need reinforcement to stay motivated. The congregation's participation is very high when they are involved in the implementation process and they get notoriously distracted when grades, stress or other organizations distract them. In short, when they're there, things are great. When they aren't, the whole group suffers. Congregation members are drawn to the club because of the friendships that they share within it.

**Community**- The community consists of potential members. The community may come to your events, but they won't be at your meetings. They either don't know about what your organization does, are committed to other organizations, are too busy or aren't interested in becoming a member of your group. You have to reel them in with events that directly and immediately benefit them. Treat this opportunity as your audition. Their curiosity will grow as you do more events that interest them, so make sure that you are always putting your best foot forward (not the one with the crusty bunions).

The goal is to integrate as many people from the community to the core by servicing their needs and helping them discover their strengths. As a leader, you need to constantly try new ways to understand what is on the hearts of your potential members. Try focus groups, questionnaires and everything else that says that you care about their opinions. You will set yourself apart from other organizations as the one group that is focused on the people, not on props.

–

In Leadership Success Secret # 3 — How to Create a 5-Star Organization, we will discuss what phenomenal results we received from our Meritocracy in one of the groups that I was a part of. The officers got twice the penalties and one-and-a-half times the rewards. This kept them in or quickly booted them out of the Core, depending on their effort level. We took the Spark Plugs and put them on the 'fast track' to the Core so they could see immediate fruits from their labor. They responded by working even harder for each round of promotions. We sliced their learning curve and integrated them into our system much more quickly. In turn, we also developed more committed members who were less likely to flake out on us by the end of the year. By changing around the emphasis of the organization from earning positions to putting in work, we went from "bore and snore" to "we want more!"

# SECRET #3: HOW TO CREATE A

# FIVE-STAR ORGANIZATION

*"Now this is the Law of the Jungle—as old and as true as the sky; And the Wolf that shall keep it may prosper, but the Wolf that shall break it must die.*

*As the creeper that girdles the tree trunk the Law runneth forward and back—for the strength of the Pack is the Wolf, and the strength of the Wolf is the Pack."*

*The Law of the Jungle*
*-Rudyard Kipling*

In all of my years as a student, a volunteer, an advisor and a speaker, I have had the pleasure of traveling the country and meeting thousands of student leaders. I was shocked to hear that so many leaders had the same issues and complaints about their campuses. What was even more surprising though, was how strikingly similar the successful organizations were in their beliefs and practices. This revelation taught me that **success is not at all random, but a calculated experience that is reserved for dedicated people**. There were five elements of success that were present in all of the thriving groups. They were: **Purpose, Accountability, Structure, Investment** and **Variety**. Together, they make the acronym PASIV, which is rather ironic considering that you must be everything but passive if you want to achieve anything. Nevertheless, we will use these elements as the five stars that create a 5-Star Organization.

## ⭐ #1 – Purpose

I've said it before and I'll say it again; **if you don't know the purpose of something the best you will do is confuse it, misuse it or abuse it.** Ironically, one of the things that many students do is give a detailed explanation why their organization exists. Thus they confuse the nature of their membership. Other times, when I ask two students in the same group what their group is, I get two different responses.

One may say that it is a social group. The other may say that they are a service organization. Thus, they misuse the group. And finally, although it seems impossible to believe, not everybody is in the club strictly because they love hanging around with you. People will join a group for a variety of reasons—from social status to padding their résumés. Yes, they abuse it.

The tie that binds successful organizations together is a collective understating of the group's purpose. **It is very difficult to be fully committed to something that you don't fully understand.** As sales trainer Marcel Brunel questioned, "How can we all have missionary zeal if we all don't know our mission?" Thriving organizations start talking about their purpose early in the process—teaching new members about the group's mission and vision, where they've been and where they seek to go. They give them a strong feel for the culture and the written and un-written expectations. Instilling deep-rooted values is also a great way to protect against the common problem of "mission drift," where, over time, a group carries the same name but their actions resemble no part of what their founders had in mind. By making your shared values a common part of your discussions, you will also be able to quickly recognize and correct behavior that is inconsistent with the acceptable standard.

I was the founding chapter president of a group called Student African American Brotherhood, or SAAB for short. We ensured that our mission was before us every time that we met. We printed it on the programs and we opened every meeting by standing up and reciting it as though it were our battle cry. It was the invisible hand that guided our decision-making process. When we were confronted with a tough decision that didn't necessarily have a right or wrong answer, we would ask ourselves, "Does this move fall in line with our mission? Does it put us any closer to achieving our purpose?" The proper conclusions became much easier to arrive at when we consulted our mission before we made any moves.

Your mission and vision can be as real or unreal as you want them to be. If you want to create common goals for the group to rally around, they must be the cornerstones of your existence and the frequent topics of conversations. One of the keys to being successful in walking in your purpose is to create shared goals in which everyone has a clearly defined role in bringing the vision to pass.

---

### Questions for further review-Purpose:

**As an organization:**
1. Does the group serve a purpose?
2. What value does the organization add to the community?
3. Is the purpose the same for all members?

**As an individual:**
1. Why am I here?
2. What purpose do I serve?
3. What value does the group add to my life?

---

## ⭐ #2 - Accountability

Oh my! Is this a sore topic or what? In all of my leadership seminars, the one topic that is consistently brought up as a black eye for most groups is the lack of accountability among members. Some leaders have even described their organization as a free-for-all where nobody can approach another member without creating an argument. The roles are thrown out of the window and the one that appears "right" in the end is the one with the best debating skills. Whoa there. Let's see if we can provide some solutions for this epidemic.

**Accountability is a culture, not an act.** When we see well-behaved children, we are usually very impressed. We can easily see that they come from a good upbringing. They seem to almost be self-regulating, choosing to behave according to an internalized set of values. For these children, discipline is only needed for occasional correction. It doesn't have to be used as an effort to beat them until they "act right." Is it possible to create an environment in which your members are that uh... well behaved? Absolutely.

First of all, in order to create a culture, you must have an unwavering commitment to a written standard. You can't let up or make exceptions. Here comes the crucial part—make your accountability system as visible and objective as possible. Objectivity is the key to preventing conflicts. Having an objective set of rules means that everyone is on an equal playing field and operates according to the same set of laws. **START EARLY!** Let the rules be written and agreed upon long before anyone has an opportunity to mess up. We will discuss this even more in-depth in Leadership Success Secret # 5—Motivating Members and Defeating Apathy Once and For All.

In order to make everyone feel equally valued, you must have an accountability system and a culture that empowers all members to enforce the rule without fear of backlash by strong-willed members. We had a phrase that we would repeat to members in SAAB to ensure that people wouldn't be late to meetings. When we would see a member in the hall, we would go up to him and say, "Don't forget, 7:00 pm sharp. SAAB *time is on time.*" That was our commitment to the culture and we stuck to it. Ten minutes into every meeting, one of the officers would say, "Alright fellas, *SAAB time is on time,*" and people who were late or did not dress in our customary shirt and tie that day had to stand up, say their name, apologize and explain why they fell short of the standard. Imagine that, young men holding each other to the highest standards and apologizing when they messed up. It was a beautiful thing.

There were some challenges though. Not everyone could handle being "called out" and tried to make a mockery of the process by mumbling or making a joke to get the heat off of them. Because we didn't have any provision for smart-alecks, we sometimes would let them get away with their antics. But we missed the fact that doing so decreased the value of the tradition. In retrospect, we should have instituted a zero-tolerance policy before it became too common. The good news is that because it was a common goal among us to maintain punctuality, we were very successful overall. The ritual is alive and well even today.

I sure hope you are seeing the big picture here. The reason why we were triumphant in this area is because we had a *process* for everyone to follow – every last one of us. So when the time came around for someone to be called out, nobody could start getting mad and claim that we were out to get him. Like it or not, it was an inextricable part of our culture. If you didn't like the "house rules," you didn't have to go home, but you had to get the heck out of our group!

---

## Questions for further review-Accountability:

### As an organization:
1. Who holds the organization accountable?
2. Is the organization accountable to its members? Non-members?
3. To what standards/rules are we held accountable?
4. By what process do we hold members accountable?

### As an individual:
1. Who holds me accountable?
2. Can I handle being "called out"?
3. At what point would I quit?

---

⭐ **#3 - Structure**

---

**The #1 way to keep good people in your organization is to have a structure that promotes growth and values their time.** Spark Plugs are always busy because everybody wants a piece of them. The last thing that they want is to be in a meeting that starts late, drags on, or fails to add value to their lives. They want to get in, get their information, and move on to their next gig. The only people who don't mind poor planning are the folks who don't have anything going on in their lives. When you ask them "what's up," their response is always the same, "Nothing much." And they mean it, too! As Zig Ziglar once joked, "Have you ever noticed that people with nothing to do always love to do it with you?" They will hang around until the cows come home because they don't have anything better to do.

To members and potential members, displaying a concrete structure symbolizes forethought, intentionality and discipline. Your organization's level of structure (or lack thereof) is just as plain to see as the gold in Nelly's teeth. Purpose without structure is chaos. Structure without purpose is—Congress. Just kidding.

Travel with me for a moment to my imaginary room in a residence hall *(Director's note: Queue the dream sequence again)*. It's during visiting hours, so you don't have to worry about curfew. There are two beds in the room, one on either side. The right side, my side, has old homework assignments scattered across the desk, clothes piled on the bed, dust everywhere and a pin up of *NSync on the bulletin board (don't laugh). The left side on the other hand, is exactly the opposite of mine. It is very well organized and clean. You could bounce a quarter off the bed because it was made so well. Based on what you have seen, what are your first assumptions about me in comparison to my roommate? Which one of us is probably more disciplined? Which one of us probably takes more pride our work? Who would you rather have as your study partner?

If you have any sense at all, you would choose my roommate over me hands down. He obviously has his stuff together. I, in contrast, am a *hot mess*. My lack of order and discipline would create the equivalent of a Six Flags amusement park for roaches. (If I did have roaches though, I would have the cool roaches, with braided antennas.)

Catch the message, boo! What's the first impression your group gives to members and potential members? Which side of the room does your group look like? And even more importantly, do the perceptions change once people get to know what's really going on behind the scenes? Once again, you see the importance of integrity coming into play. First impressions are huge for getting people to come see you. Second impressions are crucial for making them want to stay.

Here is another gift. If you want to create more structure within your organization, the best place to begin is the process by which you integrate new members. There are five phases that every potential member should go through: **Recruitment, Retention, Integration, Development** and **Promotion**.

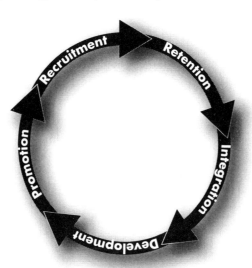

**Recruitment**- This is where potential members become members. In this phase, you seek out people who fit into the profile of qualities that you are looking for in your members and you go after them. You will learn how to create the profile for an ideal member in Leadership Success Secret #6 – Marketing and Advertising Tricks That Create Standing Room Only Crowds, so sit tight.

**Retention**- This is the toughest phase because your primary goal is to give new members enough reasons to keep coming back and eventually get involved. They are not yet emotionally committed to the group even though they may have made a financial commitment by paying dues. Using a dating analogy, they like you, but aren't ready to announce to the public that you're exclusively dating. *Don't act* like you don't know what I'm talking about!

**Integration**- Dy-no-mite! The dust has settled. They now want to get involved and contribute toward the group's goals. This is the time where they are given increased responsibilities and are fully baptized into the organization's culture. As they have proven themselves to the group, the group in turn gives them increased privileges and recognition (ie. chairing events, responsibility over key meeting functions, etc.).

**Development**- This is where it starts to get fun for you and for them as they have matriculated through the system, you have collectively established competency development goals (i.e. presentation skills, time management, networking with faculty, etc.). The organization's role in the development phase is to nurture those members and help them achieve their desired competencies. This reinforces their decision to join your organization. Can you think of a group that has done this for you?

**Promotion**- Once they have proven themselves over their current leadership roles, it's time to move them on up like the Jefferson's. The next time that elections come up, your next round of leaders will have already been familiar with their roles and will be much more effective early in their terms. They will hit the ground running. This is great news because the sooner they "get it," the sooner they can be tasked to find others that they will mentor and go through the five phases with.

If you are like I was as a student, this information would have me bouncing off the walls. I'd be ready to tear down the current structure and start all over again, trying to make the Terminator 4 of organizations. Not so fast, captain. You don't need an overhaul. The best use of your time is to first examine what you are currently doing that is working. Write it down on one side of a piece of paper. Then make a list of your weak areas and begin to formulate structures, processes and procedures that will fill in those gaps. As Michael Gerber teaches in his blockbuster book on entrepreneurship The E-Myth, "the process is the solution!" **Remember this principle, successful systems save organizations**. Having and perfecting a set of repeatable systems is crucial to the long-term success of your organization. Without a system, your organization will only be as good as the person over each event, which exposes you to inconsistent results. Conversely, a pre-designed formula will enable you to put just about anyone at the helm and still have a relatively similar outcome. Members can simply "follow the recipe," and improvise only when they have the skills to do so. **You want to arrange your group so that it is process-driven, not people-driven.**

To get you started on the right note, I have included a couple of very simple yet profound questions that you can ask yourself about your group. This will help you gauge where your group stands with its level of structure and will provide you with some specific areas of focus.

When membership is low, do you have a recruitment **process**?
☐Yes    ☐No

When members join, do you have a formal orientation **process**?
☐Yes    ☐No

What **processes** allow new members to earn increased responsibilities?

_____

_____

_____

_____

Is there a **system** for advancing mature members and making room for new members?
☐Yes    ☐No

What **systems** foster skill-building and personal development?

_____

_____

_____

_____

In SAAB, we had a big problem with finding a process that would keep people interested all year long. It almost became a tradition that the club would burn out at the end of every semester. Whereas, in the beginning of every semester we would literally have people jam-packed from wall to wall, by finals time, I remember meetings with as few as five people. Not even all of the officers would showed up! We also had additional challenges in the form of some strong personalities.

There were people who wanted to be above the law because they resented another male that was their age telling them what to do. On one hand, we were trying to keep the good people motivated and on the other hand we needed to find a way to manage the bad seeds away. We really struggled with this for quite some time. We came up with idea after idea, but nothing ever worked. Finally, we implemented a program called "Building a Brother," which was a take on our slogan, "We are in the business of building brothers."

Building a Brother was a glorified version of the merit/demerit system that the military system uses. We took a vote and decided to make the investment in lapel pins that said "SAAB" that came in three different colors. Each color had its own significance and had to be earned by participating in group activities. It was *amazing* to see how much competition and enthusiasm these pins created! It made me understand why 18th century leader Napoleon Bonaparte said, "Men will die for ribbons." The guys were doing everything they could to earn points toward their next promotion. The best part about it was that we had a public appreciation ceremony when people got upgraded to a new color, so they felt an immediate impact of their good work from the beginning. The system was a big hit all the way around.

This is a sample of the spreadsheet that our Membership Chair kept updated every meeting. Use this as a starting point for your own merit-based program. In Leadership Secret #5 — Defeating Apathy Once and For All, you will learn how to structure your program so that you steer people toward the behaviors that you encourage the most.

## Membership Point Totals

| Name | CP | CCP | DO | NS | OT | PA | LA | Total |
|------|----|----|----|----|----|----|----|-------|
| Randy | | | | | | | | |
| Marlon | | | | | | | | |
| Tito | | | | | | | | |
| Jermaine | | | | | | | | |
| Michael | | | | | | | | |

**Key:** CP=Chaired Program (+6)      OT = On Time (+1)
CCP =Co-Chaired Program (+4)     PA=Program Attendance (+2)
DO=Dressed Out Properly (+1)     LA= Late Arrival (-1)
NS= No Show (-1)

| Point Level | Subsidization* |
|-------------|----------------|
| 15 points = Orange pin | 25% |
| 30 points = Green pin | 35% |
| 50 points = Black pin | 50% |

*Note: Subsidization is financial support that the organization gives to its members. The higher your point total, the more the organization would pay for your activities. For example, if we went to play paint ball and the cost was $10 per member and you had 50 or more points, you would only have to pay $5 and the organization would pay the other half. It was our way of giving the most toward those that were the most devoted to the group.

This leads me to my next rant...uh...point. Why is it that so many of you are having one great year where membership is up and everyone is having fun, then someone graduates (or "*quituates*") and the organization sucks when they're gone? What's up with that? That's like winning the Super Bowl then ending up in last place the next year. You've got some 'splaining to do Lucy! I'd be willing to bet my Xbox that the cause of the big drop-offs is two-fold: Poor leadership development and a failure to create traceable steps. For now, I will focus on the latter: building a legacy.

Every group should create two scrapbooks each year, one with pictures, the other with processes. The process notebook should contain the president's transition log as well as checklists and evaluation from every program that you did that year. When you put together your organization's history you are making it easier to:

- Build from your current leadership for next year.
- Provide great examples of what to do and strong warnings of what not to do.
- Minimize confusion about how information should be passed on and ensure that 100 percent of the officers get 100 percent of the information that they need to immediately be successful.
- Create a legacy within your organization that you can go back and revisit years later

Again, *I have done all the work for you!* Because we now both know how important it is for you to get your processes in place, I am providing you with some sample forms that you may use for your reproducing pleasure. Consider it consensual plagiarism.

| Sample Meeting Agenda (60 Minutes or less) | |
| --- | --- |
| I. Icebreaker | 10 Minutes |
| II. Old Business | |
|     A. Officer Reports | 10 Minutes |
|         1. VP (2 min) | |
|         2. Treasurer (2 min) | |
|         3. Secretary (2 min) | |
|         4. Social Chair (2 min) | |
|         5. Community Service (2 min) | |
|     B. Cheers & Jeers | 5 Minutes |
| III. New Business | |
|     A. Member Spotlight | 15 Minutes |
|     B. Volunteer project sign-up | 5 Minutes |
|     C. Résumé writing workshop | 15 Minutes |
| IV. Adjourn | |

SECRET #3

## Sample Evaluation (For Guests)

How valuable were the program's views and concepts to you?

| 1 | 2 | 3 | 4 | 5 |
|---|---|---|---|---|

How effective was the program's format?

| 1 | 2 | 3 | 4 | 5 |
|---|---|---|---|---|

Compared to other programs on this subject area, how would you rate this program?

| 1 | 2 | 3 | 4 | 5 |
|---|---|---|---|---|

Would you attend another presentation on this topic based on what you just learned?  ☐Yes  ☐No

The idea that you found most valuable was _____

Your comments matter to us and are recorded. Please give us additional feedback.

_____

_____

_____

_____

_____

_____

_____

_____

_____

_____

_____

_____

_____

_____

_____

_____

## *Sample Program Evaluation (For Scrapbook)*

Event _____ Date _____

Program chair_____ Co-chair _____

Attendance:
Projected _____ Actual _____

Program goals
1._____
2._____
3._____
4._____

Were the goals met? Why or why not?
1._____
2._____
3._____
4._____

Key contacts used (faculty, vendors, special guests)
Name                                Contact info

_____        _____

_____        _____

Lessons learned

_____
_____
_____
_____

Evaluation form totals
1. How valuable?                    Avg _____
2. Format?                          Avg _____
3. Overall rating?                  Avg _____
4. Would you attend?                ☐Yes  ☐No
Should we do this again?            ☐Yes  ☐No

Signature_____ Date _____

Your processes are worth obsessing over. They are the physical manifestations of the philosophies that support your purpose. You could have the greatest ideas in the world, but if your systems aren't strong enough to support them, they will fail every time. Your structure must promote the values that are most important to your group (i.e. teamwork, innovation, accountability, excellence). **Ideas make things possible, processes make things permanent.**

---

### Questions for further review - Structure:

**As an organization:**
1. How reliable and consistent is the leadership?
2. Do we implement effective planning and goal setting?
3. How do we promote and reward team building and sharing ideas?
4. How important is punctuality to our organization? What does this say about us?

**As an individual:**
1. Do I have a clearly defined role that I completely understand?
2. Have I internalized the processes and adhered to the group's standards?
3. Do I offer new ideas to create more efficient ways to do business?

---

## ⭐ # 4 - Investment

It's two weeks before the Big Event and you have been tasked to get people to show up. If you were to go up to ten people and say, "The Big Event is in two weeks. Be there," and walk away, how many of them do you think would attend? Probably none. But what do think would happen if you took the same ten people to the side and asked them for their expertise about marketing, which cool faculty members to invite and other topics related to making the Big Event a hit? How many people do you think would attend this time? It's safe to say that your numbers would drastically improve because you utilized the strongest seller of all: personal investment.

On my last trip to Ohio, I saw this principle in action. I was walking to the dining hall with two student activities staff members that were responsible for bringing me to the campus. Along the way, we met one student who said that she was going to miss the program because she was going out of town to meet someone. After a short conversation with us, she saw that the workshop was going to be fun and actually said, "I have changed my mind. I'm going to the program. I'll just tell my friend to drive down here instead." When we got to the dining hall, I again saw how strong this force can be. As they introduced me to several students, I asked another young lady if she was coming to the program. I will never forget her response, "Yeah, I'm going to come, but not because of you. I'm going because I support Nicole (the staff member sitting next to me) in everything she does." Wow! What an awesome testimony of the power of influence and personal connection. It also put me in check and humbled me on the spot!

Business consultant and author Nido Qubein teaches this principle with mastery. He explains that the things that we invest in become personal to us, and what is personal to us becomes *important* to us. Unfortunately, most of us do just the opposite. We expect people to come out and support us..."just because." This is what we are communicating to others when we put up posters or hand out fliers without talking to people and telling people *why* they should attend the program. When we fail to make the event *personal* to them, we consequently fail to make it *important* to them as well. Thus, they won't attend.

The way to make your events important to people is to keep them invested in the planning process. If I can somehow get you to invest in my program, you will (even for selfish reasons) want to make sure that it is a success because you feel a sense of ownership in it. People love to see a return on their invest-ment. The more they invest, the more they care. The more they care, the harder they work, the more likely they are to show up and so on.

For example, have you ever completed a long, I mean loooong project or term paper that wore you out so much it felt like it literally took a chunk out of your behind? Would you agree that you were rather, uh, passionate about what grade you would receive? Of course you were. Your teacher had *better not* give you a bad grade for something that you worked this hard on (Not if he enjoys having usage of all his limbs). See what I mean? When your level of investment is great, so is your level expectation.

In great organizations, you will find invested people throughout the group. I am referring to people who have a sense of pride in the group that makes them feel as though it was their own. They exude zeal and passion for everything that they do within the group, even to the extent of straightening crooked posters in the hallways. They are on fire for the club! It is not by accident that this happens. It doesn't just take place overnight, either. It takes lots of time and dedication to the three most compelling areas of investment: Time, Talents and Treasures. Let's examine them in depth.

**Time**—Not some, but *all* members need to put forth and sacrifice time toward achieving the organization's goals. Time is one of our most valuable resources because we can never earn it back. So, putting time into anything (school, relationships, health, etc.) displays a certain level of commitment and dedication. We make our decisions on how we spend our time based on what we value. For instance, if people are telling you that they don't want to put in the time at meetings or service projects, they are telling you that the group has lost value in their lives. To explain this another way (get ready, we're going back to a relationship example again), have you noticed that the first sign that we show for wanting to break up with someone is that we stop wanting to spend time with them? The way that we spend our time and who we spend it with are tell-tale signs of what's on our hearts. Be careful to monitor who is putting in the time and who is falling off. These signs are indicators of your group's motivation and even your effectiveness as a leader.

*Picture this scene:* Your entire group wakes up bright and early one Saturday morning, piles into several cars and caravans down to the local shopping center where you are going to do a car wash as a fundraiser.

**Phase I: Active Involvement–**At first, you (the leader) are working hard alongside everyone else. You are all enduring the heat and busting those suds together. Everyone is rolling up their sleeves and making things happen. You are giving lots of orders, but people don't complain because they see you doing twice as much as you tell them to do.

**Phase II: Passive Involvement–**You become tired of working so hard and decide to go from work mode to management mode. Rather than doing your part, you spend your time telling your members what to do (i.e. "You missed a spot!").

**Phase III: Rebellion–**Your members realize that you're doing more talking than working and they, too, relax and slow down their productivity.

**Phase IV: Stagnation–**NO PROGRESS! Cars are backed up, your customers are wondering what's taking so long and your club is now at odds with each other, arguing about who's turn it is to get out of the shade and dry off the Ford Taurus that is starting to get water spots.

I confess. Before I understood how important my personal work ethic was to the group, I was the cause of this type of breakdown more than a time or two. This type of thing happens not only at car washes but also within your organization. When the leadership stops investing its sweat equity, the group picks up on it follows suit all the way to the dismal end. The way to prevent this mess is to always stay in Phase I. **As a leader, don't ever get caught letting people out-work you. If you want people to work harder, you work twice as hard.** Stay committed, stay focused, stay hungry. You have to be the type of member that you want in your group. Once again, may the congregation say it together, "Put the time in!"

**Talent–**Your talents are your gifts, skills and abilities. Whether it's an obvious talent or a hidden talent, everyone in your organization is talented at something. The key is to get to know your group members well enough to spot hidden talents and support them in taking the risk of trying something new. Ironically, some people can be very useful to your group but won't do anything until called upon. They would much rather wait until you ask them to do something than to volunteer themselves. It is amazing to see how much talent is inside of people that we never tap into. You may have an artist in your group that can make beautiful murals that you can use for a background at your next banquet. There may be someone that lurks in the corner, and when you get his to share one of his poems at a meeting, it brings everyone to tears. Look at your club as a vault of treasures that it waiting to be opened. Tap into that vault as frequently as possible by encouraging people to move out of their comfort zones and take on new tasks. Your organization will be much richer because of the experience.

When you get members to pledge their talents, you are tapping into a fun and exciting part of their personality. People love using their talents because this allows them to explore and expand their creative genius. Thus, people create positive mental associations and feelings about the group.

One time, I asked one of my friends who is an artist to draw some sketches for me. My only instructions were "nothing big or too time consuming." The next day, she sent me a small drawing, then for the next two days she faxed and emailed me different versions of the same sketch from different angles and poses. She wrote a note on one page that said, "I don't know why, but I am really getting into this! Here are a few more options. I couldn't sleep." I still laugh just thinking about it. When I tapped into her talent, I asked for an inch and she gave me a whole mile.

**Treasures—**People love to get their money's worth. Have you ever gone to a big party that you paid a lot of money to get into, only to find out that the DJ was wack and everybody in there was ugly? Either way, as disappointed as you were, what were you going to do? *Get your money's worth!* You just *had* to get your dance on, even if you had to dance with the "creature" that was wearing the purple suede boots. Well, maybe we're taking it a little far on that one, but you get the point.

I want my money's worth out of my organizations as well. If I give my hard-earned financial aid money to an organization, you'd better believe that I am going to get everything out of it that my membership allows. I want in on every vote, every picture taken, every T-shirt printed, and every hot wing that I am entitled to. I want it all.

For this reason, I believe in having dues in student organizations. If people don't have to sacrifice anything to get in, they won't care if they get kicked out. It is impossible for them to have a sense of respect for what it takes to be a member. They can easily develop an "easy come, easy go" attitude. I am not making a case for $1000 dues, but I do think that the dues should be something—even $10 per semester. If people complain, set up a payment plan for those that are so broke that they can't pay attention. Whatever you do, don't avoid charging dues. People will always claim to be poor, even the ones who always have their hair done and new shoes on. What I have learned is that money is just a convenient excuse for people who want all of the benefits of the organization but don't want to do anything to support it. If $2 per month for five months will keep someone from becoming a member, maybe he doesn't really want to be a part of the group as much as he thought.

While pontificating (cool word) about the virtues of investing your time, talents and treasures, don't forget to apply these principles to your school's governing body, administration, and the surrounding community. Get them to invest in you and likewise you invest in them. Become a needed resource in carrying out their agenda. If you are a part of an ethnicity—or gender-specific organization, become student ambassadors to recruit that demographic to your school. That way, your group *has* to survive, even through the tough times. The school will ensure that you survive through tough times or else they, too, will be at a loss. **If your organization isn't needed, it isn't necessary.**

---

### Questions for further review – Investment:

**As an organization:**
1. How does the leadership invest in the development of new leaders?
2. Who would be affected if we did not exist? How?
3. Are we viewed as a resource by the community?

**As an individual:**
1. Have I pledged my Time, Talent and Treasures to the group?
2. What difference am I making in my group?
3. Have I given the group my all or just enough to get by?

---

## ⭐ #5 - Variety

A little change goes a long way. It is never a bad idea to have an unexpected surprise that adds fun or value to your experience. Student organizations can get so caught up in meaningless traditions that it can almost get gross. We freely sacrifice creativity for conformity. "But that's the way we've always done it" is a good enough excuse to do the same ol' things at the same ol' time, year after year, after year, after blah, blah, blah year.

How would you like to be in a relationship in which you did the same thing every time you went out? You would want to drop your mate like a hot rock. Why then do we expect our members to show up to the same meeting location to discuss the same issues in the same format with the same people? Change it up a little. Don't be so into yourself that you forget that you're not the only person that has areas of gifting that can be useful to the group. Give other people a chance at running the show.

Actually, sharing the stage is only part of the solution. There are quite a few other ways to spice up your meetings.

Consider the following:
- Change venues for one meeting every six weeks
- Have a theme meeting (have a luau, Mardi Gras, wear school colors, masquerade, cartoon characters, 70's, 80's or 90's. The options are limitless.)
- Compete to see who can come up with the best ideas for next semester's programs
- Go see a movie and have a discussion afterward
- Invite a really cool guest speaker (hint, hint)
- Run your meeting backwards in the reverse order of the agenda
- Play a childhood game such as Duck, Duck Goose or Freeze Tag
- Have everyone bring something to share (yes folks, Show and Tell is still alive and well)
- Give door prizes to members that can tell the best lie

*Add five of your own ideas to this list, inserting your own creative flavor. Have fun with it!*

When I was in school, one of the most anticipated meetings of the year for the National Society of Black Engineers at the University of Texas was their Freshmen in Charge meeting at the end of the second semester. The freshmen got to, for one week, take over all of the roles of the officers, culminating with the meeting that they ran at the end of the week. Of course the freshmen thought that they could do everything better than the "old school" officers, so they would work hard to make it the best meeting of the year.

The laughs were plenty and the lessons were even more bountiful because the freshmen got a first-hand view of how difficult it was to handle the pressures of leadership and student life. They would also learn to appreciate the work that goes into creating a successful organization on a day-to-day basis. But above all, the entire organization got a glimpse of what its future was going to be, which was the greatest treat. It made the integration, development and promotion processes all come together at once. In one night, the future would be formed.

Kimosabe, you must be willing to break the mold if you are going to adapt with the times. Students are already tired of going through the monotony of attending the same classes every day. Be innovative. Take some risks. Don't just follow the status quo because that's the way that you've always done it. Your creativity is what will differentiate your leadership from that in years past. Separate yourself from others by doing the unimaginable. Create an environment that is a source of fun and excitement, fully charged with energy. Establish your meetings as the place to be for everyone that likes to have fun and learn something that will help them in life. Make your meetings so valuable your members will mark their calendars, looking forward to being there. If you do the same thing week in and week out, members and potential members won't feel like they're missing anything if they miss a meeting or two. Add vitality to the organization by inserting variety into your leadership. Everyone will be glad that you did.

Now that you know the five elements that create a 5-Star Organization, you absolutely must make these a part of your group *today*. Start creating processes, getting people involved and engaging your creativity. You know the framework, now it's time to get busy making the dream come alive!

---

### Questions for further review – Variety:

**As an organization:**
1. Is it possible to occasionally change up the focus, structure or tone of our meetings?
2. How can we add variety to our next meeting or event?

**As an individual:**
1. How can I benefit from being exposed to diverse perspectives?
2. Which of the following categories can I recruit people to create variety in my group:
   - Gender
   - Major
   - Hometown/geographic region
   - Ethnicity
   - Purpose for membership

# SECRET #4: DELEGATION IS A BUNCH OF B.S.

❖

Everybody says that they know how to delegate, but what most student leaders are doing is an old technique called "Dump and Run." This is where you keep all of the cool assignments for yourself and then assign the dirtiest, most time-consuming, least-gratifying work to the indentured servants that you call group members. While they are doing the grunt work, Massa runs to the big house and has a tall glass of lemonade while they sweat it out in the fields. Of course, you will get all of the glory in the end because from an outsider's perspective, you did all of the work in making the program happen. Not!

In order to be an effective delegator, you have to resist the urge to Dump and Run. Don't just tell them what to do, *show them how it should be done.* **The quality of your instructions will determine the quality of their output.** If you tell them, "This is what needs to be done," and that's it, your assignment will be subject to fluctuating standards based on whether or not the person that you delegated to takes pride in his work or has the capability to excel in this area. However, if you walk your members through the process and give them a crystal clear image of what the final product should look like, they will better understand and adapt to the acceptable standard. From there, you can build on this experience by turning it into a coaching moment where you explain to them how the task relates to the group's overall values.

Before you get back on the Complain Train again, I will verbalize your gripe for you. "But Jonathan, every time I give someone a task, I end up having to do all of the work myself. If they are going to waste my time, I might as well do it myself from the beginning." Isn't it amazing how I can read your mind? It's like I'm psychic up in here, up in here. Look, I know what it's like to feel like you have to be the owner, chef and bottle washer all in one. I know how it feels to have people disappoint you consistently, even with the smallest of tasks. On the other hand, I also know how gratifying it is to work through a problem with struggling members and show them their value to the organization in a way that they are chomping at the bit to get more involved. In the end, this is what makes it worth it to continue to work on your delegation skills.

In his book, *How to Delegate* (DK Publishing, 1998), Robert Heller explains the *five most common barriers to delegation*. They are:

1. Poor planning—"I'll do it myself"
2. Insecurity—Losing the limelight
3. Trust—People may not get the job done
4. Incompetence—People can't get the job done
5. Fear—Losing importance

As you can see, this is beginning of the acronym "PITIFUL," which is what your group will be if you don't get everyone involved. If you as the leader don't delegate because you claim to be unable to find people who are qualified, that is a warning sign that you are failing as a leader. If your leadership is plagued by fear, insecurity, trust issues or your own poor planning, you should have stopped what you were doing and begun fixing the problem long ago when you first spotted it. To find solutions, you could have asked your advisor for help, invited a guest speaker to teach on that topic, or had one of your members shadow you so they can see how the tasks should be done properly. As Heller further explains, "Your poor delegation puts you at risk of suffering some severe consequences."

---

### Consequences of poor or no delegation:

1. Overburdened/overworked members
2. Resentment of group members
3. Prevent discovering your group's strengths or hidden talents
4. Membership grows bored, disengaged, feels unneeded and sometimes leaves

Though we hate to admit it, I think that most of us can attest to having suffered at least one of these consequences during our leadership experience. Little did we know at the time that the burden of our shame rested on our shoulders. Sometimes, taking all of the responsibility can hurt us, even when we have the best intentions for the group.

Responsibility means that you are willing put everything on your sholders. **If your group is doing well, it's on you. If your group is failing and people aren't developing, it's on you.** Being the head means taking responsibility for the output of your entire platoon, soldier. With that in mind, let's take a reality check. Seriously, take a minute to really think about your answers to these two questions:

1. What will be the legacy of my leadership?
2. Who have I helped improve?

I hope that you are happy with your answers to these questions. Now, back to our talk.

I fully agree that we as leaders *should not* have to babysit people who are our age or even older to make sure that they do what they said that they were going to do. But "should" and "is" are two different things. **Though in an ideal world, we should be able to trust people at their word, this isn't an ideal world.** If we get so focused on what should be that we become blind to what is, we do ourselves and them a disservice. The only way to be effective is to deal with the hand that you've been dealt, not the one that would be better if you could change things to your liking. Tell yourself, "This is my reality. I will accept it as it is and work to make it all that it can be. It's not what I want, but it's what I have. Let's get busy."

I am a big believer in spending time talking about what we want to have, not what we are trying to avoid. So, let's start fresh. Here are some very practical tips that will help you remember what you need to be focusing on before you ask someone to give you a hand.

### The B.S. of delegation:
### 1. Be Specific

Tell your members *exactly* what you want, the deadline and why it's important to the project. Establish the timeline and checkpoints up front. Most importantly, before you end the conversation, ask them, "Is there absolutely anything that you are unclear about?" Then get them to repeat their instructions back to you to ensure that they've got it down pat. The more questions you ask, the greater your chances of successful delegation. You've got to inspect what you expect!

Before you depart from the conversation both of you should be clear on:
1. What needs to be done
2. When it needs to be done by, and
3. Why it's important

### 2. Be Supportive

We all like to hear people say, "I believe in you." Let them know that you saw something special in them and that's why you want to utilize that strength within the group. Remind them that you're behind them 100 percent. Encourage them with sentiments like, "Even if we stumble along the way, we'll just dust ourselves off and keep trying. We're a package deal." It will produce unbelievable results. Be sure to inform them of the importance of their task to the overall objective so that they feel significant and valued. People will break their necks not to let you and the group down.

### 3. Be Sparse

Once you've given them the ball, let them run with it. It is okay to ask, "How's it going," or "What are you learning?" It is *not* okay to sweat them down when you see them in the cafeteria. Back off and let them come to you—they will be more receptive to your advice if and when they need it.

Here is how good B.S. delegation sounds in real life. Let's create an imaginary scene from a popular movie *(Director's note: Queue that dream sequence again)*. Here's a sample conversation:

> **Cameron:** Lucy, Drew, we've got ourselves another mission on our hands. Let's divide up these items that Charlie told us to get for the trip. Lucy, you're good with getting anyone to do anything for you. We need you to distract that guard and get the keys to the speedboat. Cool?
>
> **Lucy:** Consider it done.
>
> **Cameron:** Drew, you're the numbers girl. You go to Angel's Bank and get $1 million for our spending money. Don't forget how we like it, small, unmarked bills. Are we clear?
>
> **Drew:** I can't do Angel's Bank, remember? We almost burned it down during our last mission.
>
> **Cameron:** Oops! Almost forgot. Make it Bank Bosley. I'll be responsible for getting our outfits. You know we've got to look good when we fight crime.
>
> **Lucy and Drew (together):** I *know* that's right!
>
> **Cameron:** Alright girls, everyone back here in exactly two hours. Send pictures to my cell phone every 30 minutes to confirm your status. Lucy, no boat, no mission. Drew, no money, no mission.
>
> **Lucy and Drew (together):** No fly clothes, no mission!
>
> **Cameron:** Angels on three. One, two three...
>
> **All:** ANGELS!

Let's get back to business. Dogonne it, use some sense! **When you delegate, don't wait until it's showtime to check and see if they did the work.** Establish checkpoints along the way that are indicators of pending success or failure. If someone is screwing up in Stage 1, don't wait until Stage 10 to see if they have followed through, then freak out when things don't turn out right.

Last Thanksgiving, my family did the impossible—we actually had Thanksgiving dinner in the same house. My mother was recovering from a hip replacement surgery that she'd had a few weeks earlier, so her time as Master Chef was limited. She had to settle for yelling out instructions (and relationship advice, and complaints) from her Lazy Boy in the living room. (To her credit, she did sacrifice her own body, dicing, cutting and seasoning a big portion of the meal before we got there...and it was *good* mama! It really was). Anyhow, we had a big problem. She was the only one who knew how to carve the turkey. What was a group of hungry black folks going to do? Our first thought was to have everyone simultaneously grab the part of the turkey that they wanted and have a turkey tug-of-war. Nah, too primitive. My brother decided to give it a shot, trying to remember Cliff Huxtable's lessons when he let Theo carve the turkey for the first time on *The Cosby Show* (I know you remember that episode).

At the end of a five-minute mauling that Jason Vorhees or Michael Myers would have been proud of, there lay a turkey that was certainly...well...cut up (to his credit, I was pleasantly surprised with my brother's efforts. Hey, I ate it, didn't I? And it was good man...it really was). We all learned a valuable lesson about delegation that evening. Though it was very efficient to let mom do all the work, in the long run, everybody lost. It would have been more effective to let everyone step up to the plate and have his or her turn learning a new skill. Had we all chipped in, we would have eaten and gotten back to watching football much sooner. By the way, next holiday, we're eating KFC.

In your club, if one of your people falls short, it's partly the member's fault for not doing the work and partly your fault for not staying on top of them. In a corporate scandal, one employee's bad decision can get several managers above him or her fired because the managers are given responsibility for all of the actions within their group—the good, the bad and the downright foul. It's not fair, but leadership isn't always fair. Get over it and move on, shall we?

*"I would rather have one percent of 100 people's efforts than 100 percent of my own."*
*-Dale Carnegie*

Use this sample event checklist as a starting place to create a program planning guide of your own that will be applicable to your circumstances. The key idea is that everyone's efforts are documented on paper and can't be left undone without someone else noticing early.

| EVENT CHECKLIST | | |
|---|---|---|
| **Event:** | **Date:** | |
| | **PERSON RESPONSIBLE/DUE DATE** | **SIGN OFF** |
| <u>Two weeks prior</u> | | |
| Facility request form | | |
| Posters created and posted | | |
| Catering established | | |
| Guest hospitality (pick up/drop off) | | |
| Hotel reserved | | |
| Reception area reserved | | |
| Security | | |
| Evaluations created | | |
| Appreciation gift purchased | | |
| <u>Day of event</u> | | |
| Pick up food | | |
| Clean meeting venue | | |
| Pick up guest's check | | |
| Evaluations | | |
| Appreciation gift | | |

*NOTE: This checklist is BY FAR not comprehensive enough to be effective. This is only a sample for you to build on. You must take the time to create a similar form that meets your group's individual needs. Your checklist should be about one page long. Leave nothing to the imagination. This is your recipe for success. Don't leave out any of the ingredients, no matter how small.*

As I look at this checklist, I think that this can be a solution to many of the problems that are killing your organizations. Some people complain about not having anything to do and those who have things to do don't do them. This system will solve all of that. There is something special about being held accountable in writing. Once all of the tasks are laid out on paper, it is much easier to delegate evenly across the group. If your officers' names are in 90 percent of the boxes (the "I'll do it myself" approach), you know that your group is too top-heavy and needs to work on building the next generation of trustworthy leaders. What's more, for those that are not handling their business, the blank spaces next to their names will be an obvious indicator that they are hurting the club. When you have this "proof," it makes it much easier to hold slackers accountable for specific actions rather than having to say, "You're always messing up." They can't argue with these checklists. If they didn't do the work, it's there in black and white. You will be able to make more educated decisions in the future about who you can trust with certain tasks and who you can't. Again, if you can't measure it, you can't manage it.

## Group tasks together.

When you have a large task before you, whether it is an annual pageant or cleaning up an auditorium, divide the big job into little chunks. If necessary, break the chunks down into chunkettes to make sure that everyone can get involved. Make sure that everyone has something to do, no matter how small the task. The only tasks that you cannot delegate are your core job functions, such as setting strategy, approving expenditures, etc.

Most importantly, *know your people!* Before you assign tasks, think about what skill sets will be required. Don't just give someone an assignment because the job is cool and you owe him a favor and appointing him will keep him off your back for a couple of days. Stop and think, will this task require strong people skills, organizational skills, project management or critical analysis? Make sure that you don't embarrass yourself and everyone else by not thinking things through and putting the wrong people in place.

SECRET #4

## Don't just dish, teach!

Lookie here, I really hope that you have received the meaning of this chapter. It is not acceptable for you to say that there are not enough good people in your organization and proceed with doing everything on your own. **If you aren't creating new leaders, what is the purpose for your leadership?** In case you missed it the first time, it's in you, my friend! You are the thermostat that controls whether the group gets hot or fizzles out. Don't get so caught up in doing things that you forget about the people that are making the "things" come to pass. If you put Robbie over making the Kool-Aid and he doesn't make it and you end up having to do all of your stuff and make the Kool-Aid on top of that, you're not helping Robbie any by doing his work for him. If you graduate and Robbie still doesn't know how to make Kool-Aid, the group will struggle in that area again next year. Of course, making Kool-Aid is just an analogy that can be used to symbolize what happens when skills are not passed down correctly. This void will reflect negatively on you as a leader. I repeat, the most telling sign of your leadership isn't what happens while you are there, but what happens after you are gone.

I know, I know. The responsible person inside of you finds it hard to watch the group flop right there in front of your face. It hurts you to see your group go down in flames, just like it would hurt a parent to watch her child get in a car accident. That's why you're such an awesome leader, because you *don't* let this type of stuff happen when you're in charge. But you've got to let it happen sometimes. You've got to let your people learn the tough lessons by experiencing the harsh realities of failure. If you continue to shield them from experiencing the agony of defeat by doing all of the work, they will never become mature leaders themselves.

Every great leader has experienced a lot of good and a lot of bad. It is the bad times that make us strive harder, plan better and work our tails off to make sure that we don't get in that mess again. It's a part of every group's developmental process that can't be avoided. You are doing them a huge disservice by making them miss out on the consequences of their actions. Just sit back sometimes and let them take their lumps. They will ultimately thank you for it.

Delegation is a science as well as an art. You need to understand the mechanics as well as the motivation that inspires people to follow through with their tasks. Trust me, there will be *plenty* of times in life where you will be tested and retested over this subject, so it's best to get all of your mistakes out of the way early so that you can be a master at this later in life. If you try to take the ball and run with it every time, you will end up wearing yourself out prematurely. Instead of your members supporting you, they will laugh at your demise. Been there, done that.

I teach students to follow this simple rule: **the first semester is about growing. The second semester is about giving**. As you get acquainted with your position and finally settle into a rhythm, you should always have your eyes peeled for the next person to fill your position. Make it your business to pour into that person for the entire second semester. Become his or her teacher, mentor and friend. The more you teach, the better you understand what you are doing. It will also highlight some additional areas in which you need to continue to grow...and this is a good thing. By the time that you complete your term, you will have established a new set of valuable skills and will be a top candidate for a higher position.

This is where having strong processes come into play. If you take the time to document everything that you do and make a "recipe book" of your procedures, the next person that you train to step in the kitchen will have a much faster ramp up period. Being a good teacher has tons of benefits, none of which equal the fact that when they learn how to do your work for you, **you can get twice the work done in half the time**! Have you ever wanted to clone yourself? Well, this is how you do it without having to move to Europe and pay for that expensive surgery. You will have less stress and more free time to spend on the important things in life, like getting more financial aid so you can eat less Ramen Noodles and Spamwiches.

# SECRET#5: HOW TO MOTIVATE MEMBERS AND DEFEAT APATHY ONCE AND FOR ALL

*"Real leaders take crap, turn it into fertilizer and make things grow. Anybody could take something that is successful by nature and manage it. All it takes is staying out of the way. A real leader takes a bad situation and makes it a good situation."*
*-Dr. Dana Carson*

I'll bet about 98 percent of you bought this book just for this leadership secret! I already know where you're coming from. Every leader has had to climb Motivation Mountain. Unfortunately, most of us got half way up, hit a bump and slid right back down. In this chapter we'll not only talk in depth about motivation, but also how to effectively discipline members and encourage the right behaviors. I know that this is a hot topic, so I will do my best to be as thorough as possible. Deal?

## How to lay the smack down!

So much for being sensitive. Before you lay the smacketh down, you have to understand who you're going to smack and why they are receiving the big beat down. All problems are going to fall in one of two categories: **people problems or purpose problems.**

1. **People problems**- Everyone is clear on what they need to do, but you A) don't have enough people, B) have people in the wrong positions (working outside of their strengths) or C) the people that you have in place don't have the capacity to get the job done.

2. **Purpose problems**- You have the right people in the right positions, but collectively you lack focus and direction. You have the ability to get the job done, but things always seem to go awry.

Do you know which types of problems are more prevalent? The answer: purpose problems. Purpose problems come about because of another important leadership principle that you need to dedicate to memory: **an organization will take on the characteristics of its leadership**. Your members will simply play "follow the leader." If the leadership is lazy, disorganized, negative, inconsistent or apathetic, the same qualities will show up in the members. Yeah, let's go there right quick.

Let's say that you're in the grocery store and hear a whiny kid screaming at the top of his lungs. The first thing you ask is, "Where the heck are his parents?" Why? Because the kid will only act out as much as the parent allows him to. **So as this relates to your group, you need to know that your club's performance, good or bad, is a direct reflection on your leadership skills.** Whether your group sucks or it's known as the place to be, take a bow, because ultimately you are the one responsible. If discipline is an issue, you absolutely must start early (even if you are reading this in the middle of the semester) and establish a standard of excellence within the club that is adhered to at all times by all members, even you. Especially you!

Your members will test you to see how much they can get away with. The moment that you start accepting excuses is the moment that the group begins to head toward mediocrity. Trust me, if you set your standards high, members will meet them as long as you give them the right amount of support and resources. **Your people will live up to or live down to the acceptable standard. The choice is yours.**

I can hear you saying it right now, "Jonathan, we have rules, but nobody follows them!" To that comment, I respond with this hypothetical question: If a policeman sat and watched a bank being robbed and did nothing to arrest the robbers, who is more at fault, the robbers or the policeman? Of course the policeman is more at fault. Robbers are supposed to rob, that's why they're called robbers. It's in their job description.

The policeman is at fault for not enforcing the rules that were already in place to penalize people who steal. **Rules only have power if they are applied. A rule without a consequence is not a rule at all. It is only a request.** Real rules have teeth, and they'll bite you in the butt if you don't follow them. This is why it is so important to be consistent with discipline. As soon as you let me get away with something, you have set a precedent. I will always be able to pull out of my back pocket that famous phrase, "but LAST time..." Then it becomes subjective (you vs. me), not objective (my actions vs. the standard).

Before we get ahead of ourselves, you need to learn the two premises for prosecuting people. These are the two criteria that you can lean on when you need to discipline someone.

### They are preference or policy.

1. **Preference**- You do something that I don't like. Your personality makes me uncomfortable.
2. **Policy**- Your actions are out of line with our standards. Allowing this to continue poses a threat to our standard of excellence.

| Preference | Policy |
|---|---|
| Subjective | Objective |
| Me vs. You | You vs. The rules |
| Attacks who you are | Addresses what you have done |

The key to success is to make the conversation about what they did, not about how you feel about them. They knew what to do and chose not to do it, thus they have to suffer the appropriate consequences. Emphasize that it was a choice they made. At the end of the day, it's all about RESULTS, not effort. When a married couple wants to have a baby, they are focused on their ultimate success, not their attempts (though this is one of the rare cases where their attempts do have their own benefits). You get the point though.

By enforcing policy, you are strictly doing your job. This is why it is so important to have measurable standards. If they can excuse themselves by saying, "I was only kinda late" or "I almost have everything that was required," you bounce back to being subjective and operating on a "good enough" standard. Be very black and white with your rules. Accept no "gray" or make circumstantial judgments. Either it is or it isn't. "Kinda" means NO. Only "yes" means yes. Take out the middle ground and watch how much easier it becomes to enforce important rules. **If you make one exception, you invariably will have to make another, if not for them for someone else.** The easiest way to shut this down is to have a "zero tolerance" policy that challenges people to step up rather than crank out excuses.

My experience has been that as long as everyone from the Core members to the visitors abide by the same rules, people won't fight when it's time to face the music. As a matter of fact, it is amazing to see even some of the most hard-headed, strong-willed members become self-correcting when they know that the group isn't playing about the rules. They will only go so far to test you. Once they see that you won't budge, they straighten up and get with the program.

Here is a sample conversation of how taking the right perspective in a tense situation can make the difference in the outcome.

**Example-**At a service project, Chien has his shirt untucked, which is a violation of the acceptable standard that the Ya-Ya Brotherhood made for themselves. Muhammad sees this and steps to Chien.

> **Muhammad:** Man, you always wear your shirt untucked. You know you're wrong for coming to the project representing us like that. Tuck your shirt in!
> **Chien:** Dude, you'd better back up. I'm not the only person who has his shirt untucked. You just singled me out because you don't like me. If you have a problem with me, why don't you say so instead of being so nit-picky about everything I do?

### Let's get ready to RUMMMMBLE!

What went wrong? For starters, Muhammad began by saying "you." Statements such as "you always" and "you never" are not effective when you're trying to get someone to do something for you. Muhammad's attitude was also very rude and authoritarian. He seemed like he was disgusted by the sight of Chien. Would you respond positively to someone with that tone of voice? NOT!

Finally, Muhammad made it a "me vs. you" battle. He made it personal, so the argument was one that he had to win so that he could prove that he was right. The untucked shirt became secondary to Chien's ego.

Let's see what happens when we clean up our little attitude and try that one again.

> **Muhammad:** Hey man, would you mind tucking that shirt in? Don't forget about our pledge of excellence.
>
> **Chien:** What about everyone else?
>
> **Muhammad:** I am going to talk to them next. I came to you first because you were closest to me and also because you set the example for the group. When they see you do the right thing, they will follow you and handle their business, too.
>
> **Chien:** You know I hate this stupid rule, right?
>
> **Muhammad:** I know. I don't like all the rules either. If you feel that strongly about it, come to the officer's meeting and make a motion to have it changed.
>
> **Chien:** Whatever. I'll think about it.
>
> **Muhammad:** Cool. I appreciate it, man. You know that the younger and more impressionable members are watching you, so thank you for being a good example.

Ahhhh...how refreshing. Wasn't that better? Didn't it sound great when Muhammad stayed focused on the rules, not on small-minded bickering? Did you catch the compliment that Muhammad gave to Chien when he said that he was an example and even thanked him for his compliance? Can you do this? Absolutely you can. And when you do it, it will make all the difference in how people respond to you.

***The keys to effective discipline are predetermination, equality and consistency.*** All of these qualities must be present in order to be successful.

## Predetermination
The system must be predetermined and established long before anyone has an opportunity to do anything wrong. If everyone agrees with the policies from jump, there is no room to complain when things go wrong in the middle of the semester. If someone misses the target, it's not the target's fault.

## Equality
Equality is important to ensure that everyone feels as though he is on an equal playing field, which means that everyone has the same shot at success. The last thing that a volunteer organization needs is for a group of officers to play a game of "we can, but you can't." If anything, the consequences should be doubled for officers because they set the tone for the rest of the group. This also keeps them humble and gives them a healthy fear of the rules. If members see that even the officers face occasional disciplinary measures, it sends a very clear message that everybody is subject to being called out when out of line. Thus, the rules reign supreme in the club.

## Consistency
Consistency is the key to keeping the peace. **100 percent of the rules must be followed 100 percent of the time, no matter what.** Nobody is above the law. Excuses can't be tolerated. I will admit that many people have criticized me for being far too rigid about upholding policies. I'm sorry, but I have seen too many occasions where being nice or letting someone slide by doesn't pay off. Being afraid to stand up for yourself and the rules because you don't want people to get mad and quit will ultimately hurt you. So I'm sorry if I come across as a drill sergeant (actually, no I'm not sorry), but I know from experience what works and what doesn't. I have learned that

when you selectively enforce certain policies, the determination of who is right and who is wrong goes to the side that can produce the fiercest argument. In essence, it makes it possible for people to be in the wrong and get away with it as long as they can argue better than the person holding them account-able. Doesn't that sound rather barbaric to you? "Me strong. You weak. Me right. You wrong." What's worse, sporadic enforcement also makes the rest of your policies void. If they can lie, skate and intimidate their way out of trouble with one rule, wouldn't they challenge all the rules? Two concessions invariably call for a third. Let your "yea" be "yea" and your "no" a "HECK no" (pardon my language).

If you tell people not to go there and they do, there must be a consequence if your rules are ever going to be respected. And when you do bring it up, focus on the facts! Placing blame on people only creates more tension and starts fights. Facts are indisputable. Be sure to hold the whole group accountable when possible. Ask each person what he could have done to step in and help the situation. Let everyone share in the responsibility of solving your family's problems. That way, the entire group will operate under a culture of constant self-evaluation and the leaders won't be so burdened with having to be the only ones who ever call people out when something is wrong. It's kind of like when your mother would give all the kids a whuppin' when one of them broke the lamp, so everyone had a vested interest in making sure that nobody did anything wrong.

Now that you know how to show people what not to do, we can move on and talk about how to promote the behaviors that you want to see. Though it may seem like it, motivation is anything but automatic. It takes a lot of work, dedication and even intense study. In his book *Motivating People* (DK Publishing, 1998), Robert Keller gives us **five points to remember about motivation.**

1. "Measuring the workplace morale of your staff should be a continual process.
2. Lack of motivation may have many causes— do not jump to conclusions about them.

3. Inquiring into attitudes carries with it an implicit promise of reform, which must be kept.
4. You may not always get honest responses about their motivational needs.
5. Exit interviews with departing staff can give valuable clues as to what is right or wrong with your motivational management."

As you can see, keeping your members' attention is about focus, not hocus pocus. You really have to be a student of the game. Motivating people is not easy, but it is something that you can do. If you're reading between the lines though, you can see from Mr. Keller's observations that you must make monitoring the morale of your troops a constant focal point of your leadership. And don't ever forget that you must, must, must be willing to keep your word. If you make a promise to improve the organization, you absolutely have to do everything in your will to make it come to pass. Your people will not perform for you unless you are committed to them. As you can see, your credibility as well as the group's spirits is at stake. This is why Keller also gives us **five questions to ask ourselves in the midst of a breakdown.**

1. "What precisely went wrong, when and where?
2. What were the root causes of the failures?
3. When were the deviations first signaled?
4. Why were the warning symbols not acted upon?
5. What could have prevented the failures from occurring?"

These questions bring about another important fact. **Apathy can be avoided.** If we as leaders take the time to correct problems when they arise rather than complain about them, we are more likely to resolve our issues much more quickly. Use these questions to nip apathy in the bud and create the ideal culture that you want in your organization.

In my day, one of the toughest areas for me was starting events late. This caused apathy within the organization because of low turnout and created inconsistent attendance among the community. When our program flyer said 7:00 pm, everyone knew that they could show up at 7:30 or 7:45 and not miss a thing. None of us thought twice about our poor guests who were graciously spending time with us and not with their families. We were careless about timeliness. Though we were unaware of it, it reflected very negatively on us as a group. This mode of operating created an unspoken expectation of mediocrity. We felt that we couldn't start on time because people wouldn't show up on time and people wouldn't show up on time because they didn't think that we'd start on time.

When you start late, 1) Latecomers aren't penalized by missing part of the program and 2) Those that actually made the "mistake" of showing up on time are blatantly disrespected by being forced to wait until more latecomers arrive. Though you may not verbalize it, the message through your actions is "Your presence isn't enough. We will feel better about ourselves when we get people who are more important than you to fill up some of these seats." If you want people to show up on time, reward that behavior. **People are tardy because you have taught them that tardiness is permissible and accepted in your group.**

Do you want to get people to line up around the corner, long before your meeting starts? Why not serve a hot meal to your early birds? Let your actions show that you value their promptness. But if you do this, do not give any (not even a bite) to anyone who arrives late. In doing so, you will be rewarding (and encouraging) bad behavior. Or if you really want to create a stir, how about having a special raffle at the exact starting time of the meeting? If the prize is right, folks will leave class early to get in line for their tickets. Get businesses to donate big prizes if you can't afford to buy them yourselves. If you are a registered 501(c)3 ( non-profit organization), their contribution is a tax write-off, so they'll lose nothing by giving you free stuff, such as coupons for their restaurant, free concert tickets and cool giveaways of that sort. For example, if you contacted a local travel agency that has special Spring Break or summer packages tailored to students, the owner may jump at the chance to come promote her business. If you know how to play your cards right (starting with that killer solicitation letter that you'll learn how to write very shortly), you could even get the owner to donate a vacation package. A free trip to Cancun would get people to come out, wouldn't it? Of course! Again, this is only one of many ideas that will work for your group if you put your mind to it. This is one way to get big donations, but it's not the only way. You have to discern what works best for you. Yes, this does take some work, but the payoff is awesome!

## Appreciation

Everyone likes to be appreciated. Here are 25 shoe-string budget ways for you to encourage, reward and thank your members. Keep in mind though, that **what you reward is what you will receive**. Before you put together an incentive plan, ask, "What behaviors do we want to encourage and promote," then think about the corresponding rewards. Be sure to give extra points for the most crucial behaviors that you want everyone to model. If apathy is a big problem, give the biggest rewards to people who step up and chair programs. Don't forget to give big rewards to those who show up early.

Make your rewards obvious, so that people who walk in late will see that they missed something. As the youngest of seven kids, trust me, I know how much it sucks to have to sit and watch everyone else but you enjoy a treat. Yeah, I still have issues. So what?

### 25 Dirt-cheap but really cool ways to reward your members

1. A hand-written thank-you card
2. A gift certificate for an appetizer or dessert
3. Flowers (Works great in fraternities. The frillier the better.)
4. Special recognition in a meeting
5. Wash their car for them
6. Give a "captain's chair" or "throne" at the next meeting
7. Carry their bags for them for a day

8. Go to Burger King and get a crown. On it write the member's name, the accomplishment and the date. Take a picture for the scrapbook

9. Have everyone say publicly why they think that person is so great

10. Pass a trophy along every week (Make it something fun—an armadillo, an Elvis statue or something.)

11. A six-pack—of water or soda

12. An email acknowledging the member's good work on the group's listserv

13. A one-year magazine subscription

14. A book or CD

15. Have all of the group members make a poster with their picture on it

16. A calendar that reflects one of their favorite interests

17. A $10 gift certificate to Wal-Mart (Don't laugh. $10 can go a looong way at Wal-Mart.)

18. Certificates of appreciation—Make it on your computer and get a frame from the Dollar Store. If you're good, nobody will be able to tell the difference. It's all good.

19. A can of "mystery meat" (Spam, Vienna sausages, pickled pig ears, etc.)

20. An e-greeting card

21. Tons of miniature chocolates or candies in a vase decorated with puff paint (from the Dollar Store, of course)

22. Get every member to write one nice thing about that person and put the notes in a vase decorated with puff paint...you know the rest

23. Purchase stationery and pens with the group's name on it that can be given away as an incentive

24. Have several people pitch in and take the member out to lunch (dinner prices can get a little steep sometimes)

25. Do a group serenade. The cheesier the song and the more people are around, the better. *My Girl, For He's a Jolly Good Fellow, 2 Legit to Quit*, and *She's a Bad Mamma Jamma* are really good for causing a scene

When you focus on solutions as we have been, you learn how to see your problems differently. Use every challenge as an opportunity to learn something new. We've already tried whining about not getting what we want time and time again. Obviously, it doesn't work. Because we can't control other people, we can't control the outcome of every situation. Yes, people will get on our nerves. Yes, people will go AWOL in the middle of the semester for no good reason. So what! This has been happening since the beginning of time. You're not the first person to ever feel this way and you certainly won't be the last. Can you overcome the odds and turn around a sinking ship? **If there weren't any problems, your leadership wouldn't have been necessary in the first place.** This is the test of your leadership, a pop quiz to see if you really have it going on as much as you think you do. Keep tinkering with ideas until you find the solution to your problems. Don't let this make you bitter, let it make you better!

Finally, I found a special treat for you. I love the "Dummies" and "Idiots" books. When thumbing through *Fundraising for Dummies* (Hungry Mintz, Inc. 2000), I found a list that authors John Mutz and Katherine Murray composed of reasons for leaders to keep going through tough times. Several of them stood out so much that I had to include them in this book.

### *Reasons to Keep Trying*
1. You believe in your mission
2. There are people you will let down if you don't keep trying
3. The reason the group still exists still needs to be met. The mission is still unfulfilled
4. Your personal credibility is at stake
5. There are always resources you haven't tapped into, things you haven't tried, people you haven't contacted
6. You take pride in your organization, in your cause, and in your personal abilities
7. You've set a goal and you need to see it through
8. Things are never as bad as they seem and crisis is never the best place to make decisions

**Hang in there!**

# SECRET #6: MARKETING & ADVERTISING TRICKS THAT CREATE STANDING-ROOM-ONLY CROWDS

❖

If your group is like some of mine have been, you definitely don't have standing-room-only crowds at your events and meetings. As a matter of fact, the attendance numbers at most of our meetings are receding faster than a middle-aged man's hairline. We walk away every week feeling frustrated, upset, questioning our abilities leaders and/or ready to quit altogether. We get tired of people signing up and not showing up. We get tired of people not signing up at all. We just get tired. I recently wrote an article for Toastmasters International called *What to do with your Faithful Few* that I believe will really help you get focused on turning your setbacks into comebacks. Here is a synopsis of what to do when your numbers start to sag.

### *Examine why your numbers have decreased*
The old adage is still true: If you do not learn the lessons from the mistakes of your past, you are doomed to repeat them again in the future. People make decisions concerning where they spend their time based on perceived value. If your group has lost its value to many of its members, find out why. Bottle up your pride and ask yourself tough questions. *Is the leadership doing something wrong?* Sometimes even minor changes can make a big difference.

### *Speak to the seats that are filled, not those that are empty*
Nothing is more frustrating than sitting in a meeting where the presiding officer continually laments about not having a larger attendance. It tells me that he or she does not truly value my presence even though I took the time to attend. What kind of mood does that set for the rest of the meeting? When faced with an unimpressive turnout at a meeting I once attended, a great leader stood before the group and said, "For reasons both good and bad, many have chosen to do something else during this time. Though we are all busy,

you however, have demonstrated your commitment to the organization with your presence tonight. I am humbled and honored to serve men and women of such great integrity." Wow! Where do I sign-up for lifetime membership?

### Make a "hit list" of new people that you will invite to your meeting every week

Have each member of your Faithful Few create a small list of people that they know who would be a good match for the organization. Each one will be responsible for bringing someone from that list to the meeting every week. Encourage members to bring in their lists to verify that they are actively participating in the program.

### Speak to people who have recently left the organization

They will give you the best insight on weaknesses within the group. Who knows? Once you tweak, shine and polish things, they may just come back!

### Frequently trade roles within the organization

Being small and nimble is a great developmental opportunity that gives everyone a good feel for executive leadership roles. In many small organizations, you find the same people repeatedly holding the same executive board positions because others do not want the weight of the fledgling organization on their shoulders. Because people probably have to shuffle to fill several positions anyway, why not make the most of it? Let everyone trade roles occasionally to be sure to give kudos to those who step up and take the challenge.

### Have joint meetings with other clubs

Sometimes it's just good to meet in a crowded room for once, even if it's with your extended family. It is also a great esteem booster to fellowship with other organizations who have similar challenges. It feels good to know that you are not alone.

### Keep increase on your mind!

In the words of motivational speaker Les Brown, "It's not over until you win."

Before we move on to the juicy stuff, I want to make sure that we get on the same page about this whole "standing room only thing." I hope that you have caught on by now that I am really big on long-term success, not short-term victories. I want you to establish the same mindset. Anyone can get people in the door, but very few offer something compelling enough to inspire people to join the organization. **It's not about how many people you gather, it's about how many people you can get to stick.** This is the difference between a victory and triumph. A victory will have people saying, "That was cool. Let me know when you're doing it again." A triumph is when people say, "I like the way that you do things. I want to be associated with people that are this good at what they do." You are about to learn how to move from isolated victories to being able to triumph once and for all.

Let's lay the foundation of your success by establishing the reason why your club is even here. **Your organization exists for two purposes and two purposes only: to meet needs and to solve problems.** Get this in your head and in your heart. The better you become at these two things, the more successful your group will be. Conversely, if you stop meeting the needs of your people, you will lose them to another organization or activity that does.

*Here are a few examples of some common items and the needs that they meet:*

| Item | Need Met |
| --- | --- |
| Mouthwash | Dragon breath |
| Cell phone | Communication away from home |
| Fast food | People need to eat, but don't have time or money for a home-cooked meal |
| Television | Getting information, cheap entertainment |

The need that is met is the *benefit* of your club's existence. **People make decisions on which group to join (if any at all) based on which option they believe will benefit them the most.** If you want standing room only, make it your business to understand the needs of the people that you are targeting and wrap your organization or event around these needs.

To take it a step further, there are two types of needs: perceived needs and actual needs. The perceived needs are what people think they need. Actual needs are what they really need. For example, we may perceive that we "need" a Jaguar, but in actuality, we only need something with four tires and a hood that will stay tied down. As it pertains to your group, people may perceive that their need is to have fun, but their actual need is to acquire skills that will help them graduate and get a job. Ironically, if you do not meet their perceived needs, you won't get your foot in the door to meet their actual needs. We will explore more of this shortly when we discuss marketing. For now, focus on who you are. Answer the following questions as thoroughly as possible:

1. What needs does your organization meet?

_____
_____
_____
_____
_____
_____
_____

2. What problems do you solve for your members and the community at-large?

_____
_____
_____
_____
_____
_____
_____

If you are having problems with answering these questions quickly, chances are you need to stop here and do some soul searching about the organization. We are already in Secret #6 out of 7, bud. If you don't have this down by now, that's not a good thing. It may be beneficial for you to bring this book to your next meeting and ask the group members collectively what their answers are. If you can answer these questions quickly, great. You're ready to move on to the next stage. It's about to start getting juicy.

## Alright, let's talk marketing.

The four basic questions of marketing are four of the most powerful questions that you as a leader of your organization must answer:

1. Who are we?
2. Who do we serve?
3. How do we serve them?
4. What makes us different?

Whether you're trying to sell Tic Tacs or Toyotas, you will have to answer these questions before you present your product to the public. Better yet, if you don't feel ready to answer these four questions, you can take a swing at one simple question:

### Why would a student with a choice of organizations choose yours?

The reasons why someone would choose your group are the benefits of membership. Remember, we're talking about people with a choice, not those who don't have anything going on in their lives. I'm talking about the high-profile, highly-motivated, successful students that would be doing just fine even without you. Why would they choose *you*? Better yet, it may be a little easier if we turn the tables around to better understand who we are really going after. Ask yourself what the ideal member is like. What is your ideal member's attitude, drive and aspiration? All of the people on your campus that fit this prototype are called your **target market**. Write down as many reasons that you can think of that your target market would be interested in your group. No benefit is too small.

Benefits

_____  _____
_____  _____
_____  _____
_____  _____
_____  _____
_____  _____
_____  _____
_____  _____
_____  _____
_____  _____
_____  _____
_____  _____

Now here's the fun part. Circle all of the benefits that are unique to your organization. These benefits are called your **competitive advantages** over other organizations. This is what you do that nobody else can do, or at least not as well as you. Do all of your members know your competitive advantage? How about non-members? If not, know that you are not alone. This problem is common in organizations from large businesses to neighborhood groups. **Businesses spend billions of marketing dollars every year to differentiate themselves from the pack. I will show you how to do the same thing, but on a shoe-string budget.**

If your circled items are significant and compelling, that means that you have a strong competitive advantage. If not, you should be concerned about your **positioning** among other organizations on campus. Your position is where you stand among your competition in the eyes of your target market. For instance, a positioning statement could be any one of the following:

Our group is the _____ organization for students who seek to learn about how to excel in the real world.

*Fill in the blank with the one of the words below that would fit for your group.*

*Award-winning*
*Oldest*
*Least expensive*
*Only*
*Nationally/internationally acclaimed*
*Most qualified*
*Most fun*

As you look at your organization and how it compares to other organizations, it is critical that you understand your competitive advantages and how they affect your positioning. As a marketer, the two phrases that I constantly repeat to myself are, "Know thy self," and "Know thy customer." I challenge myself to have a firm grasp on my customers' needs (perceived and actual) and how I can use my competitive advantages to be the one that they choose to meet them. This is especially important to you if your organization's competitive advantages are few in number or relatively insignificant.

For instance, this is what a weak competitive advantage would look like. Your positioning statement may be, "We are exactly the same as our competition in the eyes of our target market, BUT we are the least expensive." In essence, your group and other organizations are basically the same except for the fact that you charge less to become a member. BUT, if the other group with the higher dues offers its members a trip to Washington, DC to take pictures with the president in the Oval Office and be served a steak dinner on Air Force One, guess what, your BUT isn't big enough! The other group's advantages outweigh the benefit of saving a few dollars.

There are many different ways to look at this. You can look at your present circumstances and say, "That's just the way it is. We are stuck. Nobody wants us." Or you can start getting busy today, crafting the strong competitive advantages that will draw people to your organization in the future. You may decide to do something similar to what other organizations are doing, but you must innovate and creatively do it in a manner that is more attractive to your market. McDonald's isn't the only hamburger joint in the world, but it's the only one that the majority of people in this world are familiar with. They took something common and cornered the market by adding a new twist to an old game. *Now it's your turn.*

If you want to create standing room only, you have to *construct* a strong, firm, tempting BUT. Notice I say construct, meaning that it may not all come together overnight or even this semester. A good BUT may mean tailoring your group toward honors students, having an ethnic focus or catering to international or non-traditional students. Those are great niches that have large populations on some campuses. You may not have a big BUT this semester, BUT your efforts will certainly restore vigor and purpose within your group to create one. Start slowly by studying and meeting the perceived needs of your target audience to lure them away from your competition. Keep it light. Eventually, you will be able to hook them in by meeting their actual needs. Meeting their perceived needs will get them, meeting their actual needs will keep them. You can easily turn a potential negative into a definite positive.

It's never too late. There is no shortage of people on your campus. Your resources are endless. You literally could not handle it if everyone at your school joined your group. So stop telling yourself that you can't find the people who will join your group. They're out there. People join organizations for every reason under the sun. You don't have to be the best in all categories, just focus on finding one thing and be the #1 club at doing that one thing! Be the best on the market, the first name that comes to mind when people think of a certain topic. This is called **branding**. Just as people associate Tiger Woods with golf or Xerox with copiers, you need to make your organization the first choice in your niche. Your brand can be for recreation, acquiring internships, support groups, multicultural events, etc. Whatever you want to be, the sky is the limit!

Now that you have received baptism into the world of Marketing 101, let's go back and revisit those questions one more time:

| | |
|---|---|
| 1. Who are we? | What do we **help people do**? |
| 2. Who do we serve? | Who is in our **target market**? What kind of student is ideal for our organization? |
| 3. How do we serve them? | What **benefits** do we offer to attract and keep this type of student? Why would they join? Why would they stay? |
| 4. What makes us different? | What **competitive advantages** do we offer that we can use to **brand** ourselves as the obvious choice among our target market? |

## Let's advance this discussion to the next phase—advertising.

Most people confuse marketing and advertising or consider them to be the same. As a matter of fact, I did the same thing until my junior year in college—and my major was marketing. Yikes. Well, marketing and advertising are similar, but not the same. They may look like brother and sister, but they're more like kissing cousins. Advertising is what lets people know that the product is on the shelf. Marketing is what gets people to take the product off the shelf and buy it. Ya dig?

The #1 marketing mistake that people make is creating a product and then begin looking for someone who's interested in it. This is the reason why I put this chapter on marketing toward the end of this book. I didn't want you to put the cart before the horse. As I have shown you through the previous two sections, the correct way to create lasting success is to begin with the foundation of the organization, the basic tenets of its existence. **You have to first know who you are before you can expect other people to know who you are.**

Mary Kay Ash, founder of the Mary Kay cosmetic line, said of her early experiences in developing her business, "I learned that the customer had to be *taught* how to successfully use the product." You can't teach people what you don't know! How can people get excited about an organization that even you don't understand?

When you advertise, your goal is to create TOMA (Top Of Mind Awareness) within your target market. **You can get people to do *anything*, even promote your events for you— for FREE—if you know what you're doing and you reward them correctly.** Two common myths about advertising are that it is too difficult and too expensive. Actually, it can be both, but I have done most of the work for you and assembled several advertising initiatives that have been proven successful based on the campuses that I have researched. These ideas will help you pack the house at every event. Here are some great ideas on how to do so:

## *Advertising Ideas that WORK!*

1. Have everyone in the group wear bright-colored T-shirts that say, "Program tonight. Ask me about it." When you see 20 people on campus with the same shirt, you can't help but ask what in the world is going on.

2. Create buttons that advertise the event. You can even take a page out of the radio station's handbook and give prizes or raffle tickets to random people who are caught wearing the button.

3. Design promo flyers that have coupons on one side and information about the event on the other.

4. Pass out coupons for your events with a benefit for using the coupon ($___ off your admission or FREE dessert with this coupon)

5. Create tear-off sheets on the bottom of the poster so that people walking by can read the poster then keep the little sheet for themselves.

6. Word of mouth. By far, this is the *most effective and least expensive* of all advertising.

7. Set out three rounds of posters: the first round that says only the date of the event, the second round that says the date and "It's coming," then the last round that identifies the event and all of the logistical information. By that time, people will be so anxious, they will show up just to see what the big deal was.

8. Put the event information on transparencies and ask your professors if you can do a two-minute commercial for the event before class begins. This way, you can create a personal connection by showing people your excitement about the event and answer any questions on the spot.

9. Write a press release and have the local television news station and newspaper do a story on your event. If your program is going to be for a charitable cause (i.e. a battered women's shelter or cancer research), that's even better. It is great PR for your organization and for the university. College students are sometimes perceived to be very selfish and unconcerned about the world around them. If your program can show another side of college life, you will be more likely to get picked up by the local media.

10. Buy a box of Blow Pops and attach a sticker with the meeting or event's information to the stem. Everyone is a sucker for free candy (get it...sucker).

11. Bring A Guest (BAG) contest

While all of these ideas have been proven to be effective, the Bring A Guest (BAG) contest is the my personal favorite because it is a great indicator of how well your group is developing its leaders. After all, leadership is about what? Everyone in the congregation, say it together—*Influence*. If your group's mission includes training leaders, you should be putting their leadership to the test. This is a unique way to do so. Have every member commit to bringing a certain number of people to the next function (three to five people isn't too much to ask for). For everyone that fails to influence five people to attend, they put $1 in the bag (get it...BAG contest). The stash goes to the person that has the highest number of guests. Either way, there is a winner. Either somebody walks away with a ton of money (which will encourage others to really work hard next time), or the organization wins because the attendance is *three to five times* the group's membership! That would be pretty cool, huh? I kinda thought so myself.

These are only a few of the thousands upon thousands of advertising and marketing tips that are out there. If you visit your local bookstore, you can find a bunch of "how-to" books on advertising with really great ideas. Don't ever get complacent and leave the success of your event to chance. If you begin with the right focus, your "customers," and continue to create events that they will like, you will see your organization grow like never before. Trust me, it's possible. I have seen it happen tons of times. In the words of the great inventor George Washington Carver, "Take what you've got, make something of it and never be satisfied."

# SECRET #7: HOW TO MEET POWERFUL PEOPLE THAT CAN GIVE YOU THE HOOK-UP

❖

Most student organizations are poor (All the broke people in the house say, "Yeah!"). This is because most student organizations either don't ask for money or they ask in all the wrong ways. When it comes to fundraising, the majority of groups that I have encountered are very unimaginative and very mundane, which usually leaves them very disappointed. If you are one of the disappointed when it comes to money, it's time to change your attitude about money and fundraising.

I wish that somebody had slapped me upside the head when I was a student. It is unacceptable for you to continue to eek by year after year on a wing and a prayer. Do you realize how many activities your group has missed out on strictly because you couldn't afford it? Are you aware of how much more effective you could be in your community service if you could sponsor a bus of kids to come to your school for a day of SAT prep classes and a party afterward? Or what if everyone in your group was able to go on an annual leadership retreat at one of the nicest resorts in your state for two full days of teambuilding and fun in the sun? Wouldn't that be fun? Why doesn't it happen now? **Because you can't afford it!**

Enough. I just wanted to give you a picture of the possibilities, so that you would get just as mad about not having any money as I am about you not having any money. Actually, I'm not mad at you. I am mad at the mentality that has brought about chronic poverty in our student-run organizations. Just getting by can't be okay anymore. You've got to switch that mentality off if you want to do more for your group. We go to school so that we can get a good job and make "good money," but that doesn't mean that we can't start making money—"good money," right now!

In this chapter, I am going to share with you a couple of pretty cool ways to do more than your current budget says that you ought to be able to, you will learn a fundraising idea that can make you thousands of dollars. Finally, you will learn how to say thank you in a way that makes people want to keep giving you money. I'm going to put on my coaching hat and get serious about this because I really want you to get this. The potential is endless, but only if you turn off the voice in your head that says, "That's impossible" and focus on the voice that says, *"I'm going to make it happen!"*

## A Case for Co-Sponsorship

Regardless of whether your group is large or small, thriving or struggling, it is always good to have friends. A Stanford University study revealed that 87 percent of our success in life will be determined by the quality of relationships that we have with people. Eighty-seven percent! The saying is true, "your network will determine your net worth." This should scream out to you that you need to really be conscious of who you are associating with. You need to find people right now that are on the fast track or have already become successful and network with them.

As a student leader, one of the best ways to forge new friendships is by working with people on projects. You can do this through co-sponsoring events with other organizations. People that are selfish, the "glory hogs," don't like to co-sponsor events because they don't like to share the credit with other people. They let their egos get in the way and they really miss out. The advantages of co-sponsorship are tremendous. Here are a few:

- Share some of your best ideas with successful organizations
- Share programming expenses and responsibilities
- Combined membership creates a packed room
- Create new friendships that can become powerful contacts in the future

In SAAB, we used co-sponsorships as a method of exposing ourselves to other cultures. Because our membership consisted primarily of African Americans, we knew that we obviously didn't represent a big portion of the campus' population. In order to expand our horizons, we intentionally sought after other groups from diverse cultural backgrounds. The experience was awesome! We learned about different religions, foods, games, everything. It added a whole new excitement to our programs and was so much better than seeing the same faces over and over again. It kept things fun, and you never knew what would happen next. It was as much fun as a slumber party when we were kids. (Do you remember "first one to fall asleep gets ice cubes in his shorts?" I *hated* that!).

One year we were all set to do our annual conference, but ran into a small snag—we had *zero money*! We put our heads together and decided to co-sponsor the event with a local web-based public relations firm that specialized in distributing information via email about the city's hot events. Due to a previous relationship that I had with the owner, he very graciously agreed to work with us. Then we ran into another snag—in order to get his help, we had to pull in a charitable cause so his services could be a tax write-off. To make a long story short, the son, moon and Earth all aligned at the same time.

We turned our conference into a benefit for a local scholarship program, so his services were technically for the scholarships, not for us. We received hundreds of dollars in free advertising and were given access to his full staff for help with promoting and coordinating the event. Best of all, we gave a ton of scholarship money to local high school kids! Keep in mind that all of this happened with *no budget*. By ourselves, we never would have been able to pull off an event of that magnitude. But with the power of what Mark Victor Hansen and Bob Allen, co-authors of *The One Minute Millionaire*, call "a dream, a theme and a team," all things worked together for the good.

Catch the message, folks! Co-sponsorships are made possible by having strong relationships with a broad range of people. As a leader, you need to always have your eyes open for new people who can play important roles in the success of your organization. Do you think it is by coincidence that government and Big Business are always very close? Big Business needs the government's help with policies, laws and tax breaks. The lawmakers need Big Business' big wallets to fund their political campaigns so that they can stay in office. Hey, it's the American way.

Now you understand why our network determines our net worth. When you think about the future of your organization, know that four words will determined whether you sink or swim: re-lay-shun-ships.

Take some time and think hard about with whom you need to network. Faculty? Businesses? Other student leaders? Before you start your search, ask yourself two questions:

1. What can I offer that can help them to get what they want?

_____

_____

_____

_____

_____

2. What type of person (in terms of title) can help me get what I want?

_____

_____

_____

_____

_____

There are some inherent assumptions within these two questions. First, I am assuming that, by this point in the book, you have taken an inventory of your group's strengths and know how to leverage them. Hopefully, you have taken "know thyself" to heart. If you don't know all that your club has to offer, you will not be able to convey it to potential contacts. **If you get fired up about what your group is doing, so will they.**

The second assumption is that you know the wants, wishes and needs of other groups on campus. Again, if you don't know, ask! Go to lunch with one of the officers. Tell him or her that you are very interested in working with the group and want to better understand its goals and challenges to see where you can step in and help. Most people will be honored that you took the time to seek them out. Just think about it, if I said to you, "Tell me what I can do to eliminate some of the stress in your life," wouldn't you pick up the phone when you saw my name on caller ID? *You'd better!*

Stop right here. Stop, stop, stop. It's time to network, network, network! Make a short list of five people that you would most like to meet and what benefit exchange the two of you can share.

| Who do I want/need to meet? | | |
|---|---|---|
| Person | What can I do for them? | What can they do for me? |
| | | |
| | | |
| | | |
| | | |
| | | |

**You must get in the habit of list-making and goal-setting. These are the secret weapons of great leaders.** If you write down names of the people that you want to meet, you will subconsciously gravitate toward them. Your mind will continue to create new ideas that will lead you to them. Trust me, it works. Just try it and see.

*Note: For more information on networking, I wholeheartedly suggest that you read How to be a Master Networker by James Malinchak and Joe Martin. It is the best networking book that I have ever read and will share powerful secrets that you can use instantly.*

## Thank You Letters That Keep People Giving

Before you break out the construction paper and colored pencils, let's discuss why we're doing what we're doing. We were all taught when we were little how to say "please" and "thank you." Unfortunately, that was the extent of our training. Without running the risk of sounding like an etiquette teacher from Chez Malveaux, I want to break you off a little sum' sum' about tasteful acts of gratitude. Though I am a person that loves to pour into people, the one thing that will guarantee that I don't ever give to them again is their failure to thank me appropriately for helping them. No, I don't do things just so that people will bow down and worship me, but I'm just like you, if I go out of my way to help you, I at least want to be acknowledged for my efforts. Most times, the thanks in itself is all that I need, so when I don't even get that, I feel taken advantage of. I don't want you to get cut off because you don't know how to be a grateful receiver. **If you want to become the type of person that people want to give the hook-up to, time and time again, pay close attention to what comes next.**

There is a big difference between a thank you letter and a thank you note. A note is very informal and is usually hand-written. A letter is typed and goes on letterhead. A note is very personal. A letter is very professional. So, which do you send? Actually, 90% of the time, it won't matter because most young people don't have enough home training to send either one. That's right, most people send *nothing*! But for the sake of knowledge, it depends on the nature your relationship and what they did for you. **Make sure that the service matches the appreciation.** For friends, associates, colleagues and family, a warm note on nice stationery will do. If it's strictly business, play it safe and write a letter. Use this as a rule of thumb: **if you overdo your appreciation, people will feel loved.** If you under-do your appreciation, people will feel used. When in doubt, go overboard. Nobody has ever complained to me about thanking them too much or sending a gift that was too thoughtful and considerate.

According to *The Bride's Thank You Note Handbook* (Fireside Publishing, 1995), a thank you note has four parts: the greeting, body, warm close and signature (by the way, don't make fun of me for reading a bride's handbook. I pull information from *everywhere* I can. I do it all for YOU, so don't laugh). You need to make the note as personal as possible. I can't stand getting thank you notes that are so generic that they sound like they were written months before the person even knew me. Be specific. Mention the gift by name and something about its usefulness or appearance. If the gift was a check, describe how you have used it (or plan to use it). You may even want to say something about other people's reactions to the gift.

### Sample Thank You Notes:

I. Dear Tom,
Your gift was the bomb! You've got it going on 'till the break of dawn.
Word is bond,
Ron

II. Hey Stacey,
We really appreciate your generous financial gift. Everybody is excited about spending your money. We can't wait to hit the stores! Save a couple more checks for us next semester.
Julie and the girls

III. Dear Sandy,
Where did you find such original stationery? Before we received your gift, we thought that all paper looked alike. Thank you for such a distinctive and unique gift. We had to keep an eye on it all day to make sure that none of its many admirers walked away with it!
Sincerely,
Randy

If anybody writes a note like the first two, please let me know so that I can fly to their house and drop a brick on their big toe. Obviously, only the last example was one that you would want to follow. It was very personal, witty and showed a true appreciation for the giver's thoughtfulness. **Put your heart into thanking people. Be funny, be gracious, be real!**

The book *Just a Note to Say...The Perfect Words for Every Occasion* (Clarkson Potter Publisher, 1995) provides us with several more pointers on how to really wow somebody with our thanks:

1. Focus on what they gave.
2. Ask yourself, "What made it important to me?" How do you feel about the gift or their kindness?
3. Reflect on the relationship. How does the gift reflect their personality?
4. Lay it on 'em. Tell them how they hit the tar get. Use "you" and "your" as often as possible, not "me, my and I."

Keep working at it. Writing great thank you's, just like any- thing else, is an acquired skill. It won't happen overnight, but the more people you thank, the better you will get. Hey, look at it this way, if you have that many people to thank, that must mean that a lot of people are doing good things for you. When you think about it, it's pretty cool.

If you are not into writing letters, I'll share with you a tip that has produced amazing results for me over the years. When I am in Wally World or even in the drugstore and I see a card or a toy that is on sale, I put it in my basket and keep it for a rainy day. Even if I don't know who I can give it to right then, inevitably, there is always someone who I want to do some- thing for or say thank you to. When that time comes, I don't have to go to the store. I just dig into my box of gifts and send it to them right then. Of course, you could also save up those unwanted, impersonal gifts that people give you and re-gift them—much cheaper. Either way, the benefit for them is immediate gratification. I also win because I save money by picking up cool but inexpensive trinkets (you'd be amazed at what you can find for $5 or less) and I exhibit to them how much I cherish our friendship.

You can do the same with the people in your circle. You just have to be creative. I have comprised a short list of relatively inexpensive ways to thank the people who are giving you and your group the hook up.

### 7 Ways to Say Thank You to Donors

1. Say thank you and mean it.
2. Write a thank you letter.
3. Invite them to lunch. Have the whole group attend. Keep the conversation focused on them, not each other! This is not social hour.
4. Host a special recognition dinner for donors and special guests. If your group cooks for them, the personal touch will make it extra special.
5. Give appreciation certificates. Don't go cheap on these!
6. Ask them to come and speak to a group.
7. Dedicate a special portion of your newsletter to them. If you don't have one, create one!

There is a student group named Texas Gospel Fellowship that I support through periodic financial donations. Originally, I gave to the organization only because a long-term friend of mine was the advisor and I wanted to support him in his cause (Everybody turn, touch your neighbor and say, "We're talking about relationships again."). Later in the semester, they invited me to be on the panel for their Career Day meeting, where they showcased the testimonies of successful Christian business people and entrepreneurs (Everybody turn, touch your neighbor and say, "We're talking about investment again."). It really opened my eyes to all that the group was doing. I met several very bright students that spoke of the group as though it were the best thing that happened to them in their life. It deeply impacted me to the point of wanting to further support their efforts. I got to see first-hand where my donations were going, and I felt that every penny was worth it.

Shortly after the meeting, I received a newsletter in my mailbox. It highlighted the information from the Career Day event and gave testimonials of how much the members enjoyed the gathering. The most touching part was reading their prayer list–a list of the donors. I loved the special recognition from them and felt like I needed to do more to help them out, all because they took time to put their thank you in writing.

What if you did a newsletter for your alumni? What if you established silver, gold and platinum packages that included various levels of recognition? If you establish a giving structure of $100, $250 and $500 (which really isn't a whole lot of money for people who have a job), couldn't this bring thousands of dollars to your group's bank account? YES, it's possible! If even homeless people can stand on a corner and get money, you can get paid by using your intelligence and your resources. Set your giving level at something that is realistic, yet challenging, so that donors will be encouraged to stretch and give on a higher level. Create the newsletter with as much good news about your organization as possible so that donors will see it exclusively through a positive light. If you do this properly and stack your newsletter full of positive images, your bank account will begin to grow like wildfire.

## Soliciting Businesses

Who wants some money? Of course, you do. When it comes to getting the cheddar, you have to know who has the cheese and what types of businesses will give it to you. It's much easier than you think. There are people all around you who want to put money in your pockets, but you must know whom to ask and how. Look closely at these five pointers for getting the right people on your team.

### 5 Keys to Getting Businesses to Throw Money Your Way

1. When looking for potential partners, pay close attention to local companies that advertise on your campus. Start by looking at who advertises in the campus newspaper or passes out coupons around the residence halls. They are *paying* to have access to *you*! Don't spend all your time going to the same places that all of the other organizations go. You're smarter than that. Look in all the cracks, uncover every stone. **There is no shortage of money, only a shortage of people who are willing to do what it takes to get the money.**

2. Make it as easy as possible for them to help you. Offer to pick up their donation as soon as they are ready to give it to you.

3. Be very persuasive but ultimately flexible with giving options. Be grateful for whatever you receive, even if it's less than what you were originally asking for. Never forget that they don't *have* to give you anything!

4. Business people are real people, too, so be likeable. People do business (and this is indeed a *business* move) with people they like. Be someone they look forward to hearing from. Give a firm handshake, show your Kool-Aid smile, speak with confidence and sound excited about what you're doing. Before you visit or call them, ask yourself, "What one thing do I want them to remember about me? What one thing do I want them to remember about my organization or this event?" These two questions should dictate how you carry yourself around your donors. You can do it!

5. Invite them to the event. Let them see first-hand where their time, money or services are going. This is a great opportunity to shine. Everyone in the group should pour on the gratitude. Even giving your donors a standing ovation at the end of the program shouldn't be out of the question.

### Solicitation Letters

When you're ready for the big-time and you want to raise some serious cash, a good sales letter will go a long way. There is nothing like the sensation of sending out a letter and watching the checks begin to roll in two weeks later. It's incredible! Follow these seven steps and watch the magic unfold.

### 7 keys to writing a killer solicitation letter that makes your bank account go bling, bling

1. Grab their attention with a strong statistic, compelling quote or humorous opening.

2. Make your letter focus on them, not about how great your organization is. Spend just a little time talking about yourself and the majority of your time about what you can do for them.

3. Highlight the similarities between your organization's efforts with their business' mission and goals. If you don't know what they are, ask! Look for parallels between their current initiatives and what your group is doing. For example, if they give to the Salvation Army and you are doing a program for the homeless, that equals a good match. If their community focus is on child literacy and your group is doing a foam party, let's just say that the connection isn't quite as clear.

4. Be *benefit* oriented. The radio station that everyone listens to is WIIFM (What's In It For Me). How can you show them that helping you can solve *their* problems? What will you give them that they can't get on their own? Will you give them greater visibility or grow their awareness within the community? In a best-case scenario, can you direct customers to their place of business? Companies are focused on the bottom line, which is making money. Sometimes, doing something as simple as offering them a résumé book or passing out their coupons at your program is more than enough to close the deal.

5. Be concise and clear in your request to vendors. No solicitation letter should be over one page. They've seen students' requests for years, so they will already know what you're asking for, so cut the crap and get to the point. What *specifically* do you want from them?

6. Show them the necessity of giving to your cause versus giving to others (not competitively, but because of the competitive advantages that your organization offers). If they have a limited budget for donations, they want to get the most bang for their buck with every decision. Explain exactly how their contribution will be used.

7. Remember, their "yes" or "no" will ultimately come from the relationships that you forge with the ownership or management, not how much frilly language you use. Once again, the burden falls upon you as the leader to increase your networking skills, not your ability to put fluff on paper.

Everybody say it with me, "Broke no more. More money than ever before!" You have been equipped, my friend, with everything that you need to make your bank account look like a mutual fund. While fundraising is always tough and there are no guarantees, I can assure you that the more you work at this, the closer you'll be to finding the donors that will take your organization's financial future to the next level. Put in the work once and enjoy the results for months to come.

# QUESTIONS & SOLUTIONS

❖

Along my journey, there have been several questions that continually pop up, no matter where I am speaking. These seem to be among the toughest and most prevalent issues that student leaders are facing. Rather than integrating them into the chapters of the book, I wanted to call special attention to these questions and present solutions to them, once and for all.

**Q: Our group is already small. Can we afford to enforce penalties in an accountability system and risk losing members?**

**S:** Great question. To borrow a line from the great American philosopher, Forrest Gump, member is as member does. If people in your group aren't pulling their part of the weight, chances are, you have probably been doing their work for them anyway. So, if they leave, will you *really* be losing anything? The moment that you value numbers over standards, you open the door to excuses and attitude problems. You are also demonstrating to them through your actions that you don't fully mean what you say about consequences. **You can't complain about what you allow.** If you tolerate poor performance, it's not on them, it's on *you*!

Additionally, you need to sit down and ask why your group is so small that it can't afford to lose even one person. Generally, groups that have been chronically "member-challenged" are either A) not meeting people's needs or B) meeting the needs of an audience that is so small that you have to have 100 percent of the people in that segment to bring your group up to a respectable size. If your organization is formed to serve a population of six people and three of them quit because they would rather play Playstation, maybe you should broaden your scope. If that doesn't work, consider dissolving the organization or joining forces with another group.

Here are two quick questions to get your creative recruiting mind working:

1. Which students at this school value what our group values?
2. Which students are pursuing what our group is pursuing?

These are the people that you want to target. If you cannot find a group of people that would fit in these two categories, you may have created the #1 marketing mistake—creating an organization, then finding people join it. Instead, start with the people then create the programs around them, not the other way around. Give them what *they* want, and you will find much more success.

**Q: Everybody is so apathetic! People complain about not having anything to do, but when I ask them what they want, they can't give me any straight answers. Is there any way to fight apathy?**

**S:** I hear you and I definitely feel your pain. Sometimes, trying to please the insatiable is like hitting a moving target. I used to have that problem until I truly learned what it meant to hone in on a specific audience based on them having the qualities that I needed for my organization. Apathy, or a complaining spirit, was never one of the qualities that made my list.

Stick with me on this. If you were a short-order cook and I came up to you with a plate and said, "I don't know what I want to eat, but I want you to cook something for me right now," you'd look at me like I was crazy. There is nothing that you can cook for someone that isn't hungry.

My response to this dilemma is to find the people that are hungry and know exactly what they want. Look for those that are active and appreciate your efforts. Focus on them. Give them incentives to bring their friends and their friends' friends. Before you know it, you will have grown your "warm market" (people that you bring in through previous relationships versus the "cold market" that you have no connection with) such that your events will fill up again, but this time you'll only have the good people, not the headaches. And guess what—when those old apathetic people see how much fun you're having, they will get a "craving" for your organization again.

## Q: What are the biggest mistakes that you made as a student leader?

**S:** My mistakes were too many to name. My two biggest regrets, though, were not taking more time to network with other student leaders across campus and not leaving a detailed account of how we ran our organizations.

It pains me to talk to current students that are still struggling with the same problems that we went through back in the day. Had we simply taken the time to record the detail and best practices of the year and put them in a transition log, we might have been able to save future students a lot of pain and sharply cut their learning curves. Also (very selfishly I might add), it would have given me solid material to give to people who were writing me letters of recommendation. As an advisor several years later, I was always very passionate about writing everything down—everything! My first comment when I saw my officers was always, "Where are your notebooks?" I refused to make the same mistake twice.

On the networking issue, I still wonder how my life could have been different had I connected with the top five leaders and kept in contact with them. Just think about it, they were all Spark Plugs, so success was nothing new to them. They were probably doing great things since birth and are probably doing great things now. Also, Spark Plugs know other Spark Plugs. The connections could have been awesome.

---

### Note to anyone that ever went to school with Jonathan Sprinkles:

If you are now rich, famous, or know some in the first two categories, please give me a call. I really want to be your friend.

**Q: If I had to choose just one or two skills to develop within myself in order to become a better student leader, what would they be?**

**S:** For sure, the top two qualities that I would choose if I had to set the others aside would be having great articulation and being a finisher. Being very articulate is crucial because it is through written and verbal expression that we convey our feelings, emotions, instructions and desires. Our communication is the bridge that connects the gap between our thoughts and others' understanding. The more proficient we are at communicating these thoughts, the easier we can create shared goals and a common vision. Conversely, those that do not communicate well suffer a fate that's worse than getting a bad perm. They struggle through countless arguments and misunderstandings. They have extremely tough times getting people on their side and rallying the team around them.

One day, I sat back and thought about the radical leaders from the beginning of time until now. The one commonality that bound them together was that they were all very well-spoken. People make it seem like all Dr. Martin Luther King ever said was, "Free at last, free at last," but have you ever read that entire speech in its entirety? It reads like poetry. It is beautiful! That speech alone is a classic example of how the power of words can change the world.

The second quality that I would select is being a finisher in a world of starters. There are three types of people: talkers, starters and finishers. We all know people in the first two categories, and rarely do they get our respect. I used to wonder why success seemed to find certain people over and over again, but then I realized that these people enjoy great victories because they stay in the game until they win. They don't quit! When they leave home, they don't come back until they have have accomplished their mission.

When you start something, you will end up as one of two things: either a starter or a finisher. You may think this is very rigid, but it takes that much determination and then some to get through the times when life knocks your legs out from underneath you. It is a cliché, but it's true: winners don't quit and quitters don't win.

**Q: My advisor is virtually a no-show in our organization. We pretty much have to run the show without her. Is this common?**

**A:** Yes, this is a problem that is all too common. Part of it is the advisor's fault, part of it is your fault. First let's talk about the advisors, then we'll move on to you. Actually, now that I think about it, it's pretty much all your fault. Don't get mad, 'Twan. Let me explain.

If you owned a business and one of your employees only showed up on payday, how would you handle that? You would fire his butt! So, if your advisor doesn't participate in your group, you should...well, not so fast. What you should do is follow the steps that I outlined for disciplining members within your organization. The first thing to check for is a pre-written, mutually-agreed-upon list of expectations and responsibilities that your advisor must adhere to. If you failed to create such a document, you are S.O.L.—Straight Out of Luck. If you can't measure it, you can't manage it, ya dig? Thus, you have a subjective battle of you versus your advisor on your hands. Had you established a previous covenant with the advisor, you would have been able to have a conversation about the standard, which is much easier to enforce.

Never fear, my debt-laden comrade. There is still hope. You can solve the case of the missing advisor in just a few easy steps.

**Step 1—Awareness**
Make your advisor aware that you and the group have noticed his or her absence and are missing out on valuable insight and direction because of it. Make it sincere, not a brown-nose attempt. You will look cheap and pitiful if you are kissing the butt of someone who doesn't even give you the time of day, so just keep it real.

### Step 2—Redefinition

Let your advisor know that his role will not be called advisor anymore, but Developmental Coach (ooh la la). This will provide a more focused perspective of his or her purpose in your organization.

### Step 3—Reconstruction

Sit down with your advisor and write out a list of responsibilities and expectations (that you *should have had* long before this mess got started) that clearly defines and quantifies what your organization needs. This is a two-way skreet (yes, I said skreet. It's a southern thing). Make sure that both of you communicate what you are willing to give and what you need to receive in return.

### Step 4—Implementation

Take action! Work the plan. Support and appreciate your advisor when he or she steps up the commitment level to your organization, even though he or she is busy. Everybody likes to be appreciated. Encourage the performance that you want by applauding positive behaviors.

See, it's not that hard. The only tough part is getting the courage to approach your advisor about it in the first place. Of course, if they still don't want to act right...FIRE their butt!

**Q: Our e-mail listserv has turned into a circus. When I see people in the hall, I never have time to get every-thing across that I need to, but when I e-mail information to people, I never get a response. Our communication within the organization couldn't be worse and it's making it impossible to get anything done in a reasonable amount of time. Do you have any suggestions?**

**S:** But of course I have suggestions. As a matter of fact, I even have a list of solutions. I have studied communication for years and have found that while e-mail is very efficient, it is not very effective. It is one of the quickest ways to get infor-mation out and also one of quickest ways to start an argu-ment. My sales job required that I communicate with my coworkers and customers via e-mail 90 percent of the time, so

I had to get really good, really fast at learning how to send e-mails that create a response and move people to action. Although I have messed up BIG TIME and said some really dumb things over e-mail, I did manage to learn a few very useful tips and secrets. Here are few of them:

## 8 secrets of writing e-mails that get read and responded to:

1. Don't write confidential content in an e-mail. These days just assume someone else will read it (some of us have learned this the hard way). Stay professional. If it is that juicy, just pick up the phone.

2. NEVER, NEVER, NEVER write an e-mail when you're angry! If you get an inflammatory e-mail, don't make the mistake of sending a fireball back. It never makes things better. It always ends up worse. Put the keyboard down, say your response out loud, type it, read it over again, then send it.

3. When you do respond, don't try to write the 3rd Testament of the Bible. I *hate* scrolling through five pages of emotional blah, blah, blah. Stay focused on the specific issue(s) at hand.

4. Number the points that you are making. It makes it easier for the reader to focus on your specific feelings and understand your points. Keep it to five or fewer points. Nobody has time to be reading novels in the computer lab.

### This is what a well-organized e-mail should look like:

1. ADVERTISING- When is David going to finish the first round of designs for the posters?
2. FUNDRAISING- I heard that we were still $400 short. Is this true?
3. PARTY- By what time do I need to be dressed and downstairs? Don't have me waiting on you again!
4. HOME- Is it my turn to drive this weekend, or can we sucker someone else into driving? I have some unpaid traffic tickets that I need to take care of, so I may not be the best choice to get behind the wheel.

Using this technique, people can read and respond to your e-mails faster and you an quickly see if they responded to all of your points versus having them get lost in the midst of a back-and-forth chain of e-mails. It is much easier to say, "You still need to answer #3" than it is to say, "Did you ever tell me about your decision on the party? Are you still going or not?"

5. If the subject of the e-mail changes, change the subject heading. If you're talking about the forthcoming elections, the subject line, "FWD: Check this out" probably won't help you in case you need find this e-mail in the future.

6. If your message requires action, *say so!* Watch this:
   Re: Dues due Jan 28th (Action required)
   Re: Invitation to Nikki's party (Response requested)

   While you cannot physically make anyone respond to your e-mails, using this technique will drastically increase your response rate. Let's face it, we all have more things to do and seemingly less time in which to do them. The easier you make it for people to sift through e-mails and simultaneously draw attention to yours, people will reward you by getting back with you much more quickly.

7. People, will you PLEASE stop sending jokes, poems and those stupid "forward this to 10 people and you'll receive a check for $10,000" e-mails to the listserv? Eventually, the listserv will totally lose its value and will be treated more and more like spam. If you need the money that badly, donate your kidneys.

8. All caps means what? That you're YELLING! You're not my mama. You don't have the right to yell at me. If you do use all caps, only use them to emphasize something good (i.e. "I am SO excited. I am VERY proud of you"). If you don't know how to convey strong emotion without yelling, you need to sign up for a creative writing class, because I am NOT one to accept being YELLED AT!

# CLOSING

Whew...that was fun, wasn't it! I feel like we've been on a journey together and can now say that we have earned our stripes. I said it in the introduction and I'll say it again in the closing, I'm proud of you. On top of that, I am very excited about your future as a leader on your campus, in your community and in this country. Your potential in this world is endless. Before we go, let's circle together one last time so that I can deliver a final address to you. Consider it a charge and a challenge before you are sent back into the battle. Let everyone in the congregation stand at attention with their right hand over their heart *(Director's note: Queue the patriotic music and the American fluttering American flag in the background)*.

Leaders don't do what's convenient, they do what's necessary. It may not always feel good, but when you have a vision for your life and know that you have been called to do something special, you know that you must be successful...*no matter what*. The future is waiting with open arms for the generation of select leaders who can "no matter what" their way through the transition from their dreams to their destinies. We need people who aren't afraid to stand out in the crowd by standing for something noble and feel called to be a change-agent on their campuses, in the community and ultimately their country.

My friend, it is by no accident that you have been called to this privilege of leadership. Yes, it is a privilege to speak into the lives of your peers and have them look up to you as a source of strength. You (yes... *you*) have been designed "for such a time as this" to lead the group that has been assigned to your life. You have come through the winds and rain. You have endured the storm. You have fallen down, taken your lumps and had the courage to rise yet again. It was working together for your good all along. Those hardships could have been shipwrecks, but because there was need for you right here, right now, what *could* have taken you out, only served to take you to the top. In the past, you may have lost, but you didn't lose the lessons that the situations taught you. Because of this, you now can stand boldly before your peers, comforting their fears and declare to them that neither life nor death nor things passed, nor things present, nor things to come, nor things seen, nor things unseen can keep you from collectively bringing the vision to pass!

This thing is much bigger than you and me. We are simply messengers and vessels that are to be used to spread love and bring light to dark situations. You are an answered prayer, the manifestation of what our forefathers and foremothers would sacrifice, struggle and even die for. No, you are not here by mistake but very much on purpose. There is a problem that you have been made to solve, a group of people that you were sent to touch. Your purpose is significant to more lives than your own!

The pressure to give up, minimize your vision or conform to someone else's image can steal the glorious future that is in store for you. Don't let it! That pressure is powerless against your undying passion to win with integrity. Are you man or woman enough to trade in cool points for strong character? Can you bless those that curse you, pray for those that lie on you, love those that envy you or eat supper with those that are plotting to betray you? You will have to see beyond your circumstances and walk worthy of your calling, even when the call may require that you surrender your personal agenda in favor of achieving the ultimate goal.

I am proud to call you my colleague, my co-laborer and my brother or sister. You are a miracle in motion. I look forward to traveling with you on this journey. The race won't be won by the swift nor by the strong, but by they that endure to the end...*no matter what!*

# NOTES & IDEAS-SECRET #1

❖

# NOTES & IDEAS-SECRET #2

❖

# NOTES & IDEAS-SECRET #3

❖

# NOTES & IDEAS-SECRET #4

❖

# NOTES & IDEAS-SECRET #5

❖

# NOTES & IDEAS-SECRET #6

❖

# NOTES & IDEAS-SECRET #7

❖

# NOTES & IDEAS-
# QUESTIONS AND SOLUTIONS

❖